A GLIMPSE IN THE REAR VIEW

A GLIMPSE IN THE REAR VIEW

DAVE DRAPER

FOREWORD
DAN JOHN

On Target Publications, Aptos, California

A Glimpse in the Rear View

Dave Draper

Foreword: Dan John

ISBN-13: 978-1-931046-27-5, paperback

ISBN-13: 978-1-931046-26-8, epub

First printing March 2020

On Target Publications
P O Box 1335
Aptos, California 95001 USA
otpbooks.com

Library of Congress Control Number: 2020933780t

ALSO BY DAVE DRAPER

Get Serious

Brother Iron, Sister Steel

Your Body Revival

Iron on My Mind

Iron in My Hands

CONTENTS

FOREWORD

Life does funny things to our memory. We look back at our own personal Golden Ages, perhaps a time in school or holidays with our little children, and we enshrine these moments with rosy lens and imperfect memories.

We should be thankful for those imperfect memories. Like Saint Paul said in I Corinthians, "we see through a glass darkly." We forget the bullies, the hysterical tears of an unhappy toddler and periods of loss and loneliness. Our "rear view" memories fix the order of things, clear out the mess and make logic of history.

A Glimpse in the Rear View puts us in the passenger seat as Dave Draper pulls away from Muscle Beach and from the stage of Mr. Universe. He takes us into the dungeon, brings us out to the movie set and lets us help open a gym with the Austrian Oak. He pulls the weight set from under the bed for us and leads us in sets of dips on kitchen chairs.

We meet people from all over who love the iron. We bury some of them as time moves along, and others just fade from sight. We meet the wonderful and beautiful Sharon Tate, but we don't follow her fate. This isn't once upon a time; these are real stories. Life can be sad. Life can be cruel.

Dave protects us from getting too close. Stories of hunger, isolation and desperation are hidden behind sea mist and early morning fog.

When Dave finds a human body in the ocean or discusses his multiple bypasses, he cushions us in his mighty arms. He adds a touch of humor and self-deprecation to every sad story. He turns losing cartons of Bomber Blend out the back of his pickup into a slapstick comedy scene. I will forever remember the image of him hiding in wait for the police and an angry mob covered in protein powder looking for justice.

Like J. K. Rowling's last chapter of the *Harry Potter* series, we see things darkly. She writes: "But the vapor was dense, and it was difficult to make out anybody's faces."

Memory can be dense vapor. Memories can be far more important than the present.

Dave, in full poet and prophet mode, says this brilliantly:

> *"Put the filter of time on a moment, a day or an era; add slow motion, plus your favorite sounds, apply shades of black and white with brilliant color,*

and it's all legendary, pulsing and dramatic. Nostalgia is more precious than the present, more real, friendlier and informative. Today will be more important tomorrow...next year."

There will be some who wish for more details on sets and reps and how many cans of tuna to eat. Well, Dave gives us a gem from a conversation with Zabo that provides enough information to digest for the next century (if you follow the advice!):

I asked Zabo, "What is the best exercise for biceps?"

We were buds for a long time, and went on various adventures near and far. The man was known for his simple wisdom, keen wit and adversity toward the ruins of ambition. He answered my provocative query in detail, "Curls."

I was not surprised.

I continued. "What is the best exercise for triceps...shoulders...chest... back... thighs...calves?"

He answered each question generously, patiently and in order: dips...front presses...incline presses...deadlifts...squats...donkeys.

"Anything to add?"

I was riveted.

"Yeah, train hard, don't miss, keep it basic and eat lots of chicken, fish, red meat and salads. Red wine won't hurt ya."

Pin that on your wall. Post that on your social media. Point your finger at this when someone asks what to do and say: "Do this!"

It's what Dave did. It what The Bomber did. It's what the bombers do.

When Dave finally pulls over and lets us out, we know some stories, we know some names, but, far more important, we have gained some wisdom. Wisdom comes at a high price.

Dave made it simple for us:

"Today will be more important tomorrow."

Dan John
Author, *40 Years with a Whistle*

I WAS 21

My most vivid workout memories are set against the backdrop of the Muscle Beach Gym of the early 1960s. This famous, beloved relic, once located on the unspoiled shores of Santa Monica, was relocated by the persuasion of the city council to the creepy underground basement of a collapsing retirement hotel four blocks inland. The Dungeon was comprised of the equipment that once withstood the sun and salt air of the famous Muscle Beach. It was a dark and dreary subterranean reminder of dazzling and wonderful years gone by. You'd think something beautiful and bountiful was struck down and punished for its audacious freshness and strength.

In 1963, the gym was five years old. I was 21.

Force open the door, one of two 10-foot aging guardians, clomp down two flights of stairs and there it was in all its splendor. That is, if you could see the place. A very long, steep and unsure staircase took me to a cavernous hole in the ground with crumbling plaster walls and a ceiling that bulged and leaked diluted beer from the old timer's tavern above. Puddles of the stuff added charm to the dim atmosphere where three strategically placed forty-watt light bulbs gave art deco shadows to the rusting barbells, dumbbells, sagging milk crates and splintery handcrafted 2x4 benches.

Pulleys and twisted cable from a nearby Venice boatyard, a dozen Olympic bars, bent and rusty, and tons of plates were scattered throughout the 2,500 square foot floor. Dumbbells up to 160s that rattled at broken welds added the final touch that completed what was unquestionably the greatest gym in the world.

There was a water fountain in the far corner and a john in the other corner, and both worked when you needed them. Much of the light (not much) came from two skylights of glass blocks built into the sidewalk of Broadway Avenue above the south wall.

The equipment was handmade by hunky weightlifters, not craftsmen. Lumber from construction sites was slammed together by approximating eyeballs and big hammers and nails. Stout pipes held the iron plates and were wildly welded in place to serve as dumbbells from 15 to 150 pounds. Pulleys were free-hanging, six-inch contrivances with ample lengths of cable to hoist any weight at the command of the lifter.

Oddly, the underground arena didn't have a foul smell and it maintained the same agreeable temperature year round. A few 12x12 tiles remained on the concrete floor; paint had long faded, was peeling or exposed crumbling plaster. One mirror hung, a tarnished, unframed 4x5-foot chip of glass, which seemed too old and too tired to reflect an image. Why it remained was a mystery. We had to peer, squint and study its content and, alas, give up as nothing recognizable was offered.

There were never more than 10 guys in the gym any one time, only one woman I can recall. The scene sounds pitiful, but it tells of the best gym I ever trained in. These were the moments before the first seismic shift took place. You have no idea how proud I am to have had this theater and the real-life plays that unfolded day after day as part of my experience. It's pure gold.

Here bodybuilding began, embryonic: the original, not the imitation. Exercises were invented, equipment improvised, muscle shape and size imagined and built, and the authentic atmosphere exuded like primal ooze. We were awash in fundamentals and honesty. I loved it then, the memory even more now. The magic didn't come from the pharmacist; it came from the soul, the era, the history in the making, the presence of un-compromised originality yet to be imitated.

Those years I, curiously content in getting a head start, arrived at the gym between 5:30 and 6:00 a.m. while the city slept. I like the company I keep when I'm alone: I like the sounds of silence; I like the uncluttered space. With a crowd of one, there's no one to complain or groan, no self-consciousness, no dividing of attention, no one to impress. By the time I left, perhaps three or four other creatures would descend the lonely steps and dutifully take up arms.

The Dungeon was my refuge from 1963 through '66. What kept me going without missing a beat was hope in an era where none permanently resided, bouncing around like a pinball in a jangling machine. There was no glory except a rumor of respect and reputation among the lifters' underground. People in the real world sincerely frowned at me: a musclehead, a misfit, a bewildered loser who's harming himself and isn't doing us any good either.

Man, has that concept taken a spin.

My toughest workouts took place in the middle of those formidable years. I did have training partners from time to time, and one in particular, Dick Sweet, pushed me, encouraged and goaded me to otherwise unapproachable limits.

My recollection of a late morning workout, one day among many, sets a tone of our workouts in general. On the far end of a caving rack lived the merciless set of 150-pound dumbbells, awesome in length with pipe handles and suicide welds on the ends. These unwieldy contraptions could be further enlarged by strapping five-pound plates on either end with strips of inner tube.

You got it—giant rubber bands.

Getting them together took two guys, some muscle and engineering. Getting them overhead took temporary insanity. We won't talk about the 60-degree incline bench constructed of wood and 10-penny nails wedged against the wall. Never did get a good look at that in the dark.

The first set was a growling dog, biting and snapping at the flesh. I love dogs. The second set went up like stocks in a bull market, fireworks on the Fourth of July, cheers for the home team. On the third rep of the third set, the rubber band snapped and slapped me in the face.

Some guy standing in the shadows snickered.

Shortly thereafter, a five-pounder bounced off my forehead; I saw it coming. This made me serious. I had two sets to go and no more rubber bands. A short length of rope got me through the last two sets.

Did I tell you I was supersetting? Workouts without supersets were no workouts at all. The second exercise was bentover lateral raises with 60s. The welds this time were on the inside of the dumbbells, and cracked, not dangerous but sloppy. Every third or fourth rep, the web of my left hand between the thumb and the index finger got pinched in the crack. This, too, made me serious.

Good thing there's not many nerve endings there. The blood flow was light or I'd have never finished my workout.

FROM THE GRIPPER TO THE DUNGEON

Time appears to be a cool character: unchanging, forever on the go, showing no favoritism. Yet time, upon which I never impose gender, is healing. Time forgives. My life inches along, and, I presume, yours does as well. Two steps forward and one step back. The dance of men and women doing the best they can.

I can think of few acts more profitable to growing up and becoming more than the honest, hard work of lifting weights and eating right.

I have two objectives with this book: to underscore the things you need to know and to encourage you to do them. Get rid of the notion that you need to know more and more. The learning is in the doing.

A "thing" in its beginnings exhibits undistinguishable form and imperceptible movement. And what it is, should it develop, is a marvelous evolutionary process. I'm not an historian, an archaeologist or a philosopher, but I know that bodybuilding for man began when he first stumbled upon his ego many years ago. Might and muscle building is something apart. It's for those men and women who desire to exert.

There were no courses or instructions or peer supervision. No mags. They, and later I, invented and improvised and wrestled and played… hard. The equipment grew, we grew and the effort grew. Powerlifting, Olympic lifting, Strongman competition, physical culture, fitness and physique and bodybuilding grew. High performance athletes in every sport now lift weights as they strive to become champions.

The evolution continues.

Muscle and power building are not and need never become brain surgery or astrophysics. Information here, beyond the ABCs and simple math, only leads to confusion, doubt, controversy and frustration. These conditions distract from the wonderful work at hand and confound the basic instincts and investigative courage to discover. Thus limited, one imitates instead of seeks, copies rather than improvises, becomes dull in place of shining. One stops growing in leaf, and grows only in gnarly root.

There comes a time, sooner or later, when you must listen to yourself and not those around you. You must become the student and teacher at once. Look directly to yourself and your training as the masters. If you enjoy the magazines and science and research, sip on them as one does afternoon tea. Enjoy the aroma, swirl the flavorful liquid about the palate, note the heady summaries but don't expect sustenance. That comes from you, the gym and hard work done over and over again. Insight and revelation fall like sweet rain from above on the sunniest days.

I think I can safely say that I write to a diverse audience. And though I may not pen a bestseller, my ramblings might wind up in the hands of beginners of all ages, resolute former enthusiasts, struggling mid-level bodybuilders and even a nip of award-collecting pros curious about what I have to say. With that in mind, and firmly believing the basics cannot be overstated nor simplicity replaced, I'll begin.

I walked into the picture about the middle of the 20th Century when I wrapped a skinny, childish hand around a Hercules hand gripper. It lay there with its bright red handles and gleaming chrome coils amid a heap of crushed display cartons, well-sampled wiry chest expanders and "how to" pamphlets exhibiting sketches of a handsome and rugged he-man with muscles bursting through his t-shirt. WOW. Wide-eyed and transfixed. WOW.

I was seven, in the sports department of Macy's in New York City Christmas shopping with my mother. Mom got off easy. The hand gripper was harmless enough, fit in my back pocket just right and was only a couple of bucks compared to $20 for the cumbersome basketball I'd been fondling earlier. Thanks, Ma, for that lovingly cruel steel device and the ones to follow that pinched my nose and tore hair from my head in clumps.

Queeze...Queeze. Queeze...Queeze.

That repetitious grating sound—music to my ears—became like dripping water to the senses of my family, not unlike an ancient Far Eastern torture. We all endured: I, the burn in the forearms and the anxious need to grow, and they, their loving patience and frazzled nerves.

Soon, I acquired the three-spring chest expander, the five-spring super expander and a wall-mounted bungee, pulley contraption that hung conspicuously on the kitchen wall. Dear Mom and Dad and older brothers barely noticed.

Privately and uninterrupted, I pressed on when they were elsewhere watching the black and white, as TV had just arrived on the American scene. Kitchen chairs back-to-back served as a dipping apparatus and fingertips over the doorway ledge provided a tough chinning structure for a future big back. My home gym non-compare, the only one I imagined.

Imagine a 10-year-old, the youngest in a family of three boys, who inherited threadbare baseballs and raggedy mitts and smooth, under-inflated footballs like the sorrowful, unexciting toys they were. Here kid, have fun. I preferred climbing trees, racing through the meadows and scrambling up quarry walls, only to jump into the blue water far below. Batter up, balls and strikes and touchdowns were not for me.

I remember when I was a little kid, 12 maybe, and I hung from a broomstick chinning bar in my cellar while other kids were playing baseball in the park. Nobody was there saying, "Go, Dave, go. You can do it. You look great. Pull. Pull. One more rep. That'll make your lats scream."

When the stick broke and I fell on my back, nobody picked me up. When the red vinyl and chrome kitchen chairs wobbled as I knocked out dips and accidentally built supplementary muscle as I fought to keep the chairs from tumbling, nobody suggested it was fun or even good for me.

And the muscles grew.

The mad pursuit emerged from an active kid who loved to climb trees and jump from their heights. I had a favorite limb from which I chinned, on a favorite tree I called the Monkey Tree. It was my original and personal gym that served me and me alone for years. There were two chairs in the cellar by the coal bin that I placed back to back. I performed thousands, maybe millions of dips between those old splintered chairs when I wasn't chinning on the Monkey Tree. Handstand pushups came later when strength and balance were at my command.

Now the guy down the street—the big guy who built the tree house for his kid—lifted weights in his garage after work. I heard him clanging around and saw him lift the bar over his head. Wow! Strong, and he had muscles. He likes it, I can tell. He'd wave when I went by on my bike.

Vividly I remember staring down one day at a small, immovable pile of metal neatly fixed to a 16-inch steel bar. On the barren concrete sidewalk in front of my house in Secaucus, NJ, lay my first set of weights, somewhat rusty and full of gravity. My very own purchase from a neighbor up the street: for five dollars he was released and I was hooked.

My dad and brothers looked down and nodded as I eagerly slid finger-smashing plates on and off the bar and practiced tightening the red collars with my nifty wrench. Oomph! This was for me. No one on first, no one in the end zone, no swing, miss and you're out. Just me and my muscles wherever I went. My brothers each had their own thing, my mom smiled and Dad did a shoulder shrug as he walked off. No one said "no" or "hmph."

There the weights rolled onto the scene: the bar, the plates, the collars, the wrench, the clanging, the improvised exercises and the gravity and the pain. I loved the idea of lifting weights—the height of manhood to a 12-year-old—but they weren't as much fun or as free as the Monkey Tree or even the dirty old rickety chairs in the cellar by the coal bin.

I soon hated the dinky wrench and smashed fingers caught between the cold and noisy plates and the downright uncontrollable heaviness of the mute metal.

Sheesh. I'm just a little kid. I pushed and pulled and from the corner of my eye wondered if anyone cared. No one noticed. Not once did a brother or parent say, "how cool" or "let me try." It was like I was invisible. I was lucky, really. They didn't laugh, nor did they tell me to stop that banging and clanging and get those miserable things out of the house. The nasty devices were rolled under my bed when not in use, which was next to the beds of my two older brothers. Tight quarters and tight muscles for a squirt.

I was encouraged. Self-inspiration was anonymously planted, took root and grew, freely and unencumbered.

Though I never saw his movies, a poster promoting Steve Reeves in *Hercules* deeply branded me, setting me aside for a labor of love to last a lifetime.

What I did with this pig iron, the 10s and fives and three-pounders, collars and bar, is vague and unfocused. There were no courses or instructions or peer supervision. No mags in my library.

I invented and improvised and wrestled and played—hard. I arranged and rearranged the makeshift set of weights and within a month I was fully hooked, cookin,' bombing and pumping.

WHEN IN DOUBT, REMEMBER THE PAST

I recall only bits and pieces of my pre-teen iron struggles in my wedge of a bedroom shared with two older brothers, causing me to wonder how much I trained. But these patchy images indicate the novelty of exercise was outlived and replaced by enduring hard labor. I approached my meager 30-minute bout with the iron like self-imposed detention from which I needed release. Sounds like fun for a pre-teen; how long is this boyhood infatuation going to last?

Evidently, by rummaging through wall charts and mimicking exercises demonstrated by the Brunet brothers—the muscular Canadian twins working for an aspiring Joe Weider, circa mid-'50s—I devised a routine that was worthy of sufficient repetition to cause boredom and some accompanying bumps of muscle.

I learned early on that this weightlifting stuff was not a game to be played like batter-up baseball, jump-and-shoot basketball or pass-and-run football. It was me, myself and I, crowded at the end of my bed with a stack of jangling, defiant weights that only I cared about.

My recollections picture me alone as I rolled the wobbly inert mass around the worn linoleum floor. I balanced them on end and crawled under. I pushed and pulled, curled and pressed 'em. I mightily applied the bothersome flat alloy wrench to the red collars and changed the weights from light to heavy and back again, always expecting the plates to unfix and fall on my head.

The screws left barbed gouges in the 16-inch bars.

The object wasn't cheering and scoring points, winning or losing, now or anytime soon. The purpose wasn't running and jumping, throwing and catching and bouncing off a teammate's shoulders and energy on the field in a vigorous afternoon. The motive was wishful thinking, a kid's hope, the dream—a daring image of a muscular form (me) flitting around in my little mind. Where'd that come from? Now you see him, now you don't.

My next cast-iron memories include a pair of dumbbells and a bar next to a mattress in the basement, two chairs back-to-back for dips and a splintery wooden chinning bar rigged across overhead beams. I'm 15 and the Weehawken High School coach calls me "Arms" when he sees me. He's cool. I'm quiet. He allows me to tumble and walk on my hands while the other kids play basketball during PE.

I remember, too, a rare sight in a fancy New England prep school where kids of wealth studied for future enrollment in slick universities. Under my bed was that same barbell I slaved over in the basement in Jersey. It was a curious thing in the dorms of Avon Old Farms, where tennis racquets, jai-alai gear and pictures of home hung on the walls next to the bunks.

After studies and before lights-out, I rolled the rude iron hunk from its resting place and put it through some hefty motions. Little clinks and clanks could be heard amid the din of young teens releasing their pent-up evening energies.

Rumor had it there wasn't another barbell in all of Connecticut.

This less-than-rich scholarship student from Secaucus never saw the inside of a slick university. My older brother Jerry was about to graduate Yale when he asked me what school I was going to attend in the fall. I stared at my tuna on whole wheat, shrugged my shoulders and said, "I dunno." He said wisely, "Where there's a will, there's a way." That was the end of that conversation.

I got a job, ironically, in a metal fabricating factory and bought a pair of 45-pound plates with my first paycheck. Leroy Colbert stashed them in my car.

The sequence of rusty recollections increases and clarifies from there.

Now an adult-like head pops through the bog of dependent youth and I'm on my own to locate and inspect the obstacles of life. I drag the 45s up a flight to my very own one-room apartment, where they join the weights of my childhood at the end of yet another bed. The pile of steel looks impressive and I wonder if the floor to the old flat can sustain the weight. I clean and press 185, a first for me and, I'm certain, the creaking boards beneath my feet.

We're in there.

Seventeen and I still haven't read a muscle magazine. Who needs them? The wall charts are long gone and I'm propelled forward by the same imaginary forces that set me in motion a lifetime ago. Though, now, that unseen mover is settled in the unconscious halls of my mind.

The mind plays a critical role in weightlifting and building might. And instincts contribute generously, if we let them. Lifting is something we know personally and privately, a diversion, a satisfaction, a voice, an instructor, a secret power and a swell muscle builder. It makes smooth the rough places. Being strong is fun and enabling, impressive and protective.

At the foot of the bed, a temple of sorts in that dismal silent room, I remember doing barbell rows, stiffarm pullovers, overhead pressing and press-behind-necks, light benches, barbell curls, dips and chins and pushups and lunges. They gave it and me life. Three sets of this and that every day for eight to 15 reps seemed to work.

Some days I had it, some days I didn't; some things never change.

Focus was coming slowly, patience remained at a crawl, discipline was being ground into my skull and resolve led the barking pack. Form needed work and muscle identity and recruitment simply took time and practice—inevitable maturity. Fortitude quite naturally joined my resolve. Call it the evolution of a musclehead that cannot be hastened.

Still, the iron doesn't move without a lot of hard work and sacrifice, discipline and persistence. After a day's work, there it is...the barbell in front of the bed.

On frequent weekends, the weights were transported to my vehicle where they lay scattered in noisy confusion until they reached my out-of-town getaway. Lifting on Saturday and Sunday with no time constraints was particularly appealing; I could wallow and test myself in the tranquility of a quaint cabin (leaky shed) in the north. Getting a life had not yet occurred to me.

The weights seemed to follow me wherever I went. Not like a habit or a puppy or body odor, but like an extension of myself, my expression, my need and desire. Some kids sang or danced or sketched or played musical instruments or engaged in sports. Some did nothing in particular or hustled or got in trouble. I lifted weights as if it was my duty, my individual responsibility or private obligation.

Unknown to me, lifting was beginning to define who I was.

Then came my first experience with man and weights beyond the limited one-step, two-step lifting in the confines of a bedroom or basement: I joined the YMCA. A raucous group of guys tossed the metal around like it was a bunch of junk, in a room the size of a closet.

Corners of bedrooms, basements and garages provided the common training areas for the rare breed of lifters brewing 60 years ago. I wasn't the only one stumbling around popping his veins, although some days it seemed like I was as I look back over the muddy waters.

The YMCAs across the country all had classic weight rooms that housed barbells and benches to rival The Dungeon I'd later settle into. These undersized rooms had low ceilings with hot water pipes traveling in every direction and were invariably located in the basement next to a big boiler room.

The Y in Elizabeth, NJ, was my first gym beyond the environs of home. A good-looking Italian kid—Joey Dinetta, Mr. New Jersey at the time—invited me to train with him one summer, that he might teach me how much fun weight lifting with the boys could be. There I gawked at a seven-foot Olympic bar as if it was an oversized, outdated relic, the preposterous length of which surely must have presented a hazard to early lifters.

I discovered how to cram 20 big guys into a room large enough for 10 and how to pitch a bar into a corner, load it with weight and do killer rows. I learned how to do inclines and spot incorrectly by dropping a dumbbell on my training partner's head. I didn't understand much, but I learned enough to graduate to the big time.

I learned something about fighting for my turn on the bench and lifting more than the other guy. I learned stuff you need to learn and forget before you learn anything at all. The place was a zoo. Six months in a zoo was enough for this animal, and I left in the fall.

The Vic Tanny's in Jersey City—my next exposure to exercise beyond my innocent reality—had red rugs, chrome weights, mirrors on every wall, music and girls. I frowned, looked straight ahead and didn't make a peep. I did my first 400-pound bench press with a chrome training bar and a string of nine chrome 20s and one 10 on each side…don't forget the little chrome collars.

My first job working for a gym was as the weekend manager at Vic's, circa 1961. Friday they gave me a key and told me I started Saturday at 9:00 a.m. Imagine, 19 years old and I'm already a gym manager. I'm on my way, I'm a cool guy.

As I finished my workout that Friday evening, I felt my lats and triceps assume a permanent flexed position. It sort of hurt, but it was the price one had to pay.

Arriving early Saturday morning to take control of my domain, I witnessed a miracle. Using my new key, I unlocked the prominent glass doors at the top of the broad staircase and the gym—my gym—all 2,000 square feet, was gone.

Overnight. Where did it go? I did a series of 360s with my mouth open and it still didn't appear. Gone to the next county, no doubt. I didn't need no stinkin' gym job anyway. Tanny's was a dog-and-pony show, neither of which I am.

There was no reason why a guy couldn't lift weights and have a family, too, so I married and bulked up along with my wife, Penny. She gave birth to Jamie, a beautiful baby girl, and I'm 235 by the time I'm 21 and Mr. New Jersey.

To support a family and my growing bodyweight, I took a part-time job with the Weider Barbell Company in Union City, an aspiring enterprise fixing a hold on the swelling world of muscle. Leroy Colbert showed me how to do seated dumbbell alternates and I did my first set of squats in the corner of the small warehouse during lunch break. A kid could amass serious muscles that way.

I remember Joe saying, "You guys are always bombing it. When do you ever work? Leroy, I'm going to call Draper 'The Blond Bomber.' What do you think, eh?"

A month later, there it was on the cover of *Young Mr. America* magazine.

I'm learnin' and growin.' Weider Company goes west, and I go with them to live in tranquil Santa Monica on the alluring far edge of the earth. You might say it was there where I enrolled in my first year of university: UCMB, University of California, Muscle Beach. The year was 1963.

There at Muscle Beach, as it faded off into the stunning California sunset, I met and shared with the last of the true erectors of the bodybuilding foundations: the cornerstones such as Joe Gold, Zabo, George Eiferman, Bill Pearl, Armand Tanny, and Hugo Labra, a handful of mighty men—heroes—that formed the heart of bodybuilding and lived those golden, carefree days gone by.

These men with instincts intact felt their way around the weights and equipment, lifting more and intellectualizing less. And to them I attribute a certain quality of creativity in my training and an appreciation of the fundamentals. The late 1960s have been referred to as the "Golden Era of Bodybuilding," when big men pressed on curiously, methodically, and with great concentration. During those years the various training principles were established and stand distinctly today—sound, tried and true.

One of these years I'll graduate, go out in the world and get a job. Until then, it's one course after another, day after day, learn, learn, learn, practice, practice and practice.

I have a Master's in Bombing and Blasting.

TRUE ADVENTURES

My mind faded to black as I stared at the darkened ceiling. It was the middle of the night; I'd been here before. Having exhausted all significant subjects of despair—soaring milk prices, cat pee on my Reeves poster, cancellation of *Friends,* Cubs loss of five straight—I awaited more constructive thoughts to fill my empty brain. Sleep had left the building. Finally, Lady Luck cast a charitable nod my way and I found myself reviewing the absurd extents to which I had gone in the past to accomplish my workouts. I regard such thought-processing as vital and illuminating, worthy of meticulous consideration. Further, that my recollections were clear and detailed substantiated their value and influence. I was onto something big.

I was 18, not yet in California, and by sheer will—not affluence—I owned an adorable Corvette built for two. Sometimes it was a friend and I who shared the limited yet furiously fast space; other times it was me and a rattling heap of plates from five pounds to 50 and an assortment of bars and collars—the tender things of a half-crazed weightlifter. I lived in a rented room in my hometown where I worked, played and trained.

On weekends I'd travel upstate to work part-time to pay for the Corvette and its gas, which made perfect sense at the time. Barbells were nowhere to be found upstate and I had to bring my own, which also made sense at the time.

It was hauling them down two flights of stairs from my rented room to the Vette parked in the street below that seemed stupid. But wait, it gets better. Hours later, hauling them from the Vette through an overgrown garden to the rear window of my meager weekend quarters was almost as dumb, but it meant I would at last construct the raw materials into the essential muscle-making tools so I could lift them like a maniac. I endured the dumbness for the greater good.

This went on for a summer until I came to my senses and decided to do weighted chins and dips instead. Eliminating the tedious, time- and energy-consuming hauling process enabled me to eat, go to the john, train with spirit and include crunches and leg raises as well. Great workouts, and my lats and shoulders grew wider as my gut tightened.

One must travel the long wearisome road to discover the shortcuts.

I trudged on, up one slope and down the other, weights in tow.

Not a whole lot of time passed before I found myself in California training with the big dawgs. And that I did, grew some more, and soon returned home to compete in the Mr. A., which I won.

That trip, I stayed briefly with kindly friends on the far side of middle-aged who knew nothing about iron and steel. I was now a big boy from California, very healthy and tanned too. It was late summer and record heat and humidity consumed the east coast. The home where I was staying was small and air-conditioning only served the tiny master bedroom, not the basement quarters where I temporarily stored my weights.

One day, the kindly retired couple was gone—a drive in the country—and I had the house to myself. That is, me and my newly resurrected 100-pound dumbbells and a wobbly three-in-one Weider bench. Oh, boy! One set of flat presses next to the washer and dryer had me on my knees, panting and sweating. It also had me imagining what a delight it would be to breathe the cool air one flight above.

Did I mention I'm compulsive and selfish and single-minded? The staircase was narrow and rickety, and I had my doubts as I hauled the hundred-pounders up the steep ascent. I'm bad! We made it, all of us: bench, dumbbells, small transistor radio playing rock n' roll, jug of water and me, eyes like quarters.

I'm selfish, as admitted, but of the non-intrusive variety. I'm respectful and careful and considerate and responsible and honest. Honest. I was meticulous in the moving process and certain there was no damage to the household. I'd ask permission, but the dear hearts are not here. They'll never know. I felt sneaky.

My exercise plan was clear: as many sets of flat presses as I could accomplish, followed by plenty of sets of stiff-arm pullovers and concluding with one-arm dumbbell rows until I dropped.

This was paradise, though I'm wedged between the bed's maple footboard and a set of matching dresser drawers. Nice rug. The dumbbells were unwieldy, and being cramped irritated me until a car pulled in the driveway. It's them and they brought friends along too.

I flipped. They'll flip. What do I do now?

I tried desperately to disappear, but failed. The windows were stuck shut with age and paint. Too late to hide, I said, "Frankie, hi. . .you're home early. I was just..."

Frankie was fast and said, "What the heck are those things? Is that what you had in the basement under the staircase? I tried to move them with my brother last Christmas and we thought they were bolted to the floor. How'd you get them up the stairs? Kitty, Sonny, Millie, come here. Look at this. He carried those things upstairs, those black weight things. Too hot down there for ya? Yeah, too hot in the car, too. Let me see ya move one of those; whatta ya do with 'em, roll 'em? Geez!"

I moved my mouth like I was going to say something intelligent, but rockin' Frankie was on a roll.

"Show Sonny and Millie your trophy…kid won Mr. America Saturday in New York City. What do ya do with those things, lift em? Let me try and grab one."

"Here," I said, as I reached down, grabbed the rascals, pulled them to my knees and sat down, "you start like this."

They were impressed, eyes bulging. I rolled back, gave the black clanking beasts a thrust to the overhead starting position and said without a grunt, "And then you press them like this."

The adrenalin from their shocking arrival and my need to amaze them gave me a few extra reps. I got 10 or 12 beauties—swoosh through the air and the metal was down and on the floor like a pair of swans on a silent and still pond.

Sonny marveled, Millie shook her head and Kitty made iced tea. Frankie hung out and held my knees down while I did stiff-arm pullovers, expecting me to burst or rip my arms from my body. I completed my rows with the door closed to keep the cool air and the huffing and puffing to myself. My spectators, bored with my antics, drank iced tea coolers in the shade on the patio. They took the transistor with them tuned in low decibels to Your Hit Parade.

The weights were left under the bench at the foot of the bed—ready to go—until I left town at the end of the week. I felt sad returning them to their secret place under the old house. Those rusting beasts of burden lay in the dark gathering dust another year before I returned to test their gravity. A dandy space had been cleared in a cool corner of the cellar and a large fan sat before the same old bench. How thoughtful.

I was the resident musclehead.

And I shiver to think I was almost the resident musclehead in a California jailhouse only a month before my triumphant return.

Beachball Dan's leather hat factory was nestled in one of those metal pre-fabs constructed on a slab in a day and a half. Very cool, but you can access the tin containers with a can opener or a screwdriver. Dan was a lifting buddy and had his Olympic weights, platform and racks conveniently set up and partitioned off in the rear of his shop.

It was Sunday; the shop was closed, I wanted to work out…and I had a screwdriver. Within 10 minutes I squeezed my 240-pound body between loosened corrugated steel sheets and was standing before a bar loaded with iron, a very metallic scene. Then the cops arrived. How did I know the joint was rigged with an alarm system?

"Hold it right there, buster. Don't move a muscle. How far do ya think you're gonna get with those weights?" said the man in blue.

"I don't know. It's only my third set and I'm still warming up," I said without grinning. Dan came in within 30 seconds and smoothed things over. We worked out together for another hour before hitting the smorgasbord downtown. I paid.

Real weightlifters have big hearts.

That's us, bombers: A little nuts, but big hearted, high flying and unstoppable.

WHERE HAVE ALL THE COWBOYS GONE?

I first met Joe Gold when I moved to California in 1963. I was a 21-year-old Jersey boy and Joe was a 41-year-old Californian. We were down in the Muscle Beach Dungeon where light was sparse, scattered and dim. I was performing weighted chins and dips in slow supersets when Zabo introduced me to his longtime friend, the Gold. The two were like the head and tail of some rare coin: very different and very much the same. They stood side by side in what was the common attire of Muscle Beach muscleheads—cut-off sweats, flip-flops and well-worn T-shirts.

I hate flip-flops, wore cheapo Keds and was right in style with the rest of the gear.

Joe was talking about building a gym in Venice that would "get the guys out of this hole in the ground." I couldn't imagine any place in the world that could be better than the Dungeon. It was a perfect, dark and ominous mess. Sacrifice and pain were inscribed on its cracked walls and toughness was inhaled with each breath of stale air.

"Joe's got a hunk of property a block off the beach," said Zabo in his disconnected Jersey accent. I didn't know much, but from the looks of these two leathery mutts, I was not about to give up my precious membership to the Muscle Beach Gym that day. They're cool, but I wondered if they could build a sandcastle in wet sand.

I also wondered if they could get any tanner. They lived for the beach and had trained on it for a hundred years before some saps from the city came with a legal technicality and a bulldozer and took it all away: a spirit, a culture, a way of life, an expression and a freedom.

I missed the real deal, but the memory was so thick, I absorbed what was left from the men who hung on, wouldn't let go…couldn't let go. These two were the quintessential Muscle Beach bums, bronzed, healthy, muscled, strong, loose and free.

Both men honorably toured the South Pacific with the military during WW II and then happily toured Las Vegas nightclubs with Mae West and her showgirls in the uplifting aftermath. Live and learn from the good, the bad and the ugly.

The Joe Gold leaning against the crumbling plaster of the Dungeon wall was a man of many skills and experiences. He served in the Merchant Marine as a Boatswain and Machinist's Mate when ships were going to places of interest. He'd already built his first gym in Mississippi during an extended stay on the Gulf while serving in the mariner's world.

The equipment was handmade, robust, efficient and innovative (large pulleys, handsome oversized structures for mechanical advantage, functional adjustments), and this was barely the middle of the 20th Century.

Joe was sailing, lifting, growing, learning and onto something.

It was just another day when the three of us shared hopes and dreams in the cool depths of the Dungeon and breaking ground for the imaginary gym was at least a year away. I looked like a blimp and was yet to compete and win the Mr. America; the ground beneath my feet was as sure as the desires and plans of our muscle talk. I shrugged my shoulders, wished the sun-soaked team the best and promised I'd visit the site when I had transportation.

Zabo, my west coast mentor, told me he was helping Joe in every way he could. I knew the Chief well enough to seriously consider what help he might offer Joe: trench supervisor, nail inspector, water boy, tool attendant, time keeper, night watchman.

As I shifted into gear in preparation of the Mr. A in 1965, I saw less of the Dream Team and more of the inside of a tuna can. One day, I cut loose and brought a bag of fresh fruit—maybe it was a six-pack or two—for the boys who were finally digging the footings for the foundation of the future Gold's Gym.

Zabo was nowhere in sight, asked by Joe to dig a hole at the rear of the project. We, a muscular motley mob of five in tank tops and headbands, stood around in the late afternoon sun guzzling, gabbing and bragging and more than a little curious where Zabo was hiding.

Though I believe we all heard it, Seymour Koenig was the first to see it. In the shadow of the northeast corner was a crunch, followed by a tuft of dirt flying out of a mysterious hole. The first observation was unsure, a bit mystifying, and our eyes connected as if to say, "Do you see what I see?"

Artie Zeller reached for his Roloflex. "I gotta get a picture of this."

Joe shook his head with calm resignation. "That's the Chief; I know it. I asked him to dig a hole for a power pole and not to stop until I came back with the cement. That was this morning after breakfast. I forgot."

We edged our way over like a pack of stray dogs. Zabo looked up from a hole the size of a Buick and said, "Hey Joe, where ya been, man? How big ya want this thing? I can't get out."

By the end of the summer, we were training in a palace instead of a dungeon. The dumbbells were precise and machine locked and reclined in heavy metal racks; the Olympic bars were absolutely straight, the plates matched, were in abundance and properly placed in plate holders; the pulldowns and cables and long lat-pulls and crossovers operated with precision and big-steel solidness.

Open the front door and look out and there was Main Street, a block from the ocean. Inside were all the appropriate and perfect bars and dumbbells to sooth and develop a musclehead's body, mind and soul. Thick-handled and pristine, solid and bold, clean, visible, handy.

And look! Large and polished mirrors on every wall.

Everything was tight, balanced, smooth, even and exciting to the touch. It all fit, worked and hummed and was tailor-made by Joe Gold's own rugged hands and bright imagination and machinist skill. The benches were made of rugged steel, designed and constructed in his garage at the end of a cul-de-sac a mile away. The pulleys were oversized for smooth sailing and mounted on oversized frameworks for multiple purposes. Everything had its space; just enough, not too much. Light zoomed in from skylights and front windows by day and fluorescents by night. Showers and a restroom were in the back, above the teensy parking area. Sweet.

The arena was set for building muscle and might, and the atmosphere and attitude followed. There were no greats walking the floor and no hotshots greedily consuming the mirrors. Guys and a few gals pushed the iron with basic purity, hard work and mature passion.

Joe Gold was a very good man and was always the adult in the room. Neither jerks nor loudmouths were allowed, thus respectable behavior was integrated.

There was quiet before the storm.

MEMORIES OF MUSCLE BEACH

There's a picture that occasionally sneaks up and causes a shudder. I'm 22, 250 pounds and a newer resident of Santa Monica. I'm a donut covered with powdered white confectioner's sugar and I stand conspicuously like a grinning duffer in trunks on the hallowed sands of Muscle Beach.

It was late Saturday morning in mid-July and that picture was just the beginning. I was making friends and getting comfortable in my new world, like a mutt in a new home, tail wagging, chasing balls, yelping.

I was ready to play.

I wandered across the crowded beach to the water's edge and gazed beyond the surf and splashing kids to the tips of tiny sails racing in the distance. The rugged pier that stretched offshore stood 50 yards to my right, and the majestic blue Pacific reached for my knees with each vigorous wave.

I grew up on a lake and the sports in which I competed included swimming. Water was not my problem; it was the ocean I had not yet embraced. The restless and mighty waves fascinated me and what was lurking beneath the surface gripped my imagination.

Something about sharks caused me to pause and consider the weight of my courage and fear. My courage sank like a rock; yet fear, as powerful as it was, could not defeat my pride. I dove into the churning, seductive white waters and joined in the revelry.

The thrust of the waves and the tug of the undertow captured my attention and soon I was lost in play, my physical yearnings peaked and dared. I flopped and floundered, yielding to the sea, for in spite of its mass and muscle, it was, that day, a gentle bully.

One good thrust and one good tug sent me upended into deep waters. I rode the swell above the crowd with a grand view of the undulating, watery, people-packed beaches. Suddenly, the swell dropped me into a deep trough where all but the ominous sea walls vanished. My feet hit the sandy bottom briefly and up again I rose.

MAYDAY…MAYDAY…

Head for dry land, full speed. Negotiate the rise and fall of this formidable joy ride and head for shore, post haste.

Up and down, again and again, my adrenaline in pursuit. I rolled with the next big, wet smothering cushion and hoped it would take me to the beach. My feet once more touched the ocean floor as I drifted toward the towering pier and its breakwater protection. The exaggerated sea levels diminished, my short-lived rip tide consumption left me both energized and weary…most certainly humbled.

The great blue ocean, the vast, inscrutable and wonderful sea was not yet done with me. I thanked God as I recognized a hazy onlooker, Panic, and his assortment of devices to bring one before his Maker. Clever rascal, I thought, as I continued to grope for shore.

I was now in reach of those innocent and playful children, their screams and laughter and wiggling bodies a fantastic delight. We're in heaven for a day. I wanted to hug them, lift them and toss them like my Uncle Johnny did me at the lake. Life was never more fun.

Up and down with smaller breaking waves, I struggled with confidence and renewed energy, when my foot stepped on something slick… something large and smooth. A swell lifted me up and forward and, at last, I stood waste deep in the foaming release of the big waters.

What did I kick? What was that bulky slithering object?

I stood frozen. I was safe. I cast my eyes in its direction and wondered if it was alive. Did I encounter a shark? Was it a bather?

I scanned the surface looking for movement and saw only families of carefree swimmers. Seconds later, I was back at the spot amid the swells, breakers and undertow; looking, searching, prodding, again within the gaze of Panic…get ye behind me…There, hovering beneath my kicking feet was a large figure of a man looking up, looking still.

Down I went to grab the hulk and drag him to the surface. I fought frantically as he slid with the ocean's movements and slipped repeatedly from my arms, my bear hug of insignificant might.

We looked and sounded like the rest of the mid-summer frolickers—only he was silent. He made it to the water's edge where I dropped him on the wet sand.

My lungs ached as I lie on the wet sand like miserable debris. I saw stars and thought wildly. The man, his lungs didn't ache. No stars, no thoughts.

Lifeguards added oxygen and electricity, two hours too late. Nobody knew him. He jumped off the pier early that morning, so they say.

Probably around the same time I was posing for that dumb picture.

THE GOLDEN, CAREFREE DAYS GONE BY

Bodybuilding as we know it today began some 80 years ago when men like John Grimek and Steve Reeves lifted weights in preparation for the first Mr. America title in the late 1930s. The famed Muscle Beach emerged in Santa Monica in the '40s.

And, as I recollect, it was in the mellow mid-50s when I lifted my first set of barbells. Little did I know the reps and sets, moans and groans that lay before me.

I was just a kid and virtually nobody was doing that sort of thing. Weightlifting and muscle building didn't have wide public appeal or approval, and 99 out of 100 athletic coaches gave it the thumbs down. There was no encouragement or inspiration from a society that considered us either stupid or egotistical, both maybe.

The two guys who inspired me to lift in those days were Anthony Petrowski and Tony Nepeerski, local dock workers with powerful arms from hard work, meat and potatoes and some gnarly weightlifting.

I arranged a makeshift set of weights and within a month I was fully hooked on lifting—barbells and dumbbells were my solid steel friends that I could trust. When the going got tough, when I kept missing the baseball, and when girls were far too cute to talk to, the weights were there and they spoke my language.

I loved the resistance they offered, and without coaching, gymnasiums or teams of players, I could enjoy a basic oneness of the activity where I was in control of being controlled.

I wrestled with those little monsters for hours on end, pushing and pulling randomly to exhaustion until patterns of exercises formed. Slowly and surely my body took shape and muscle power and size became evident, almost by accident. I knew of no muscle magazines, looked toward no competitive rewards, idols or flimsy self-gratification. Simply, the play and pleasure of painfully pressing on was my stimulus.

And, too, I admit that the exclusiveness and loneness of the adventure have a quality that reaches to the marrow of my bones.

In high school I wrestled a bit, worked on the high bar and swam competitively, but it was the weights that buoyed me up. A job with Weider Barbell Company lured me to Santa Monica after I won the Mr. New Jersey title in 1962.

There at Muscle Beach, as it faded off into the beautiful California sunset, I met and shared with the last of the true erectors of the bodybuilding foundations—the cornerstones such as Joe Gold, Zabo, George Eiferman, Bill Pearl, Armand Tanny, Clancy Ross and Steve Reeves, a handful of mighty men—heroes—that formed the nucleus of bodybuilding and lived those golden, carefree days gone by.

These men, with instincts intact, felt their way around the weights and equipment, lifting more and intellectualizing less. To them I attribute a certain quality of creativity in my training and an appreciation of the fundamentals.

Living in Venice in the '60s was like living in a junkyard with a bunch of junkyard dogs. Biting was allowed and the food wasn't free. I had to make a living, learn and grow. My workouts served to stabilize, fortify and entertain me, but no way could I see training to beat Sergio a real wise career decision—baby needed shoes.

(As if I could have; he was from another planet.)

I found myself making rugged oversized furniture out of old wood, loving it and making enough money to pay the bills. Tranquil, alone and natural, woodworking matched my workouts. Someone could say the '70s never happened and I'd believe it.

I became a carpenter of sorts quite by accident (as is commonplace in all my pursuits). To keep me company as I sawed planks and carved wood into oversized objects of furniture, I drank a little wine and smoked a little dope.

This pattern—smoking, drinking, eating, training, carving and sleeping—kept me busy.

The world around me, but for a handful of friends and family, spun on its own familiar axis. Frank, Arnold, Mentzer—whoever—did their thing and I did mine, light years apart. I didn't ignore or neglect, judge or deny competitive bodybuilding. I simply lost interest as one does for racing cars on the boulevard or watching corn grow season after season.

My respect and affection for the guys and our experiences were cast in bronze. Creating in wood and trips to Big Sur and Mendocino became my preoccupation.

The bodybuilding world expanded; it appeared to grow tentacles and I found it alien to my perception of muscle and might. I dug the metal: the single-mindedness, the struggle, the intense body feelings, the pump and burn and heat and sweat, the battle, defeat and mostly the victory, the wordless communication and knowing amid a very small tribe and the muddled or vacant stares I captured from puzzled, stumbling on-lookers—the rest of the world, really.

Not so much an ego trip as an amused ape, comfortably aware of itself.

I came to understand that staying big and muscular and strong was inherent and a chosen function for my new passion to build my large wood forms. The egocentricity I shared primarily with myself was fulfilling and harmless enough. As far as I could see, the world nearby was kicking itself up and down the freeway and maybe I could help by not participating.

In 1970, after winning Mr. World in New York City, I sensed a shifting of the gears in bodybuilding and stepped out of competition. The sport took off like a rocket to the moon, soaring into the '80s with ever-increasing momentum.

Allow me to sneak within a few thin pages a sufficient discourse of my life out to pasture between the years of 1970 and 1985. The weights never left my side, no more than a good old sheepdog leaves a gritty sheepherder tending the south 40. I trained every morning with fire in my gut before the cock crowed.

Got along fine with the bird; 'twas the people who presented me minor distress.

Somewhere, halfway through the '70s, my family and I escaped from the expanding yet deteriorating Los Angeles scenery to settle like toadstools in the midst of the Santa Cruz redwoods. Heaven, one would conclude, a dream come true: a wooden house in the middle of 12 wooded acres, lovingly cultivated by God Almighty.

Not quite.

I saw my family depart and my sinister, cynical companions—drugs and alcohol—lead me from my home to a barren gardener's shed in a little orchard on the edge of Nowhere. No power, no running water, no bucks, no buddy.

Hey, I still had the weights, was still lifting, never stopped. Commendable.

Add to that: the booze and dope stopped. Suddenly.

But not until after, at one point in 1983, so did my heart.

The doctors and staff at the Dominican Critical Care Unit treating me for acute congestive heart failure expected my life to cease as heartbeats strained and repeatedly failed. Three weeks after this bout, I was wheeled out the side door to resume my tortuous journey.

My eyes cleared and I looked at the black and white and smoldering landscape around me, silent ashes. If I didn't do one good thing each day, I still plugged into the gym and resuscitated my soul.

Two years of one day at a time, sets and reps, iron and woodwork therapy, fear and trembling, prayer and God, and I stood upright.

Unbeknownst to me, bodybuilding was about to be exploited, big-time. There was money to be made accompanied by greed, power and frenzy. Muscle mags resembling catalogs appeared prodigiously. Merchandise, apparel, miracle supplements for overnight muscle, equipment of every description, gym chains, mondo contests and promoters swamped the fields of green.

Lo and behold, I joined the gold rush.

No, not really. I did, however, determine to get out from under the hooves of the stampeding horses. One fine day in September 1989 in the corner of Santa Cruz, a small gym opened its doors, freshly painted and filled with new equipment. The banner read "World Gym" in large print, my name in the corner along with the hours of operation.

February rolled around and Arnold arrived in a police-escorted limousine followed by Joe Gold and a Hollywood-style Venice entourage. We had a grand opening and I established a long-term relationship with the World Gym gang.

Scotts Valley nestled five miles away became home to a second World Gym planted by my partners and me two years later.

And today muscle building has continued to gain amazing popularity worldwide, both as a sport and as a way of life. The image associated with muscles has been appropriately lifted and the respect and appreciation a bodybuilder deserves is clear.

Big muscles have become big business.

Moms and dads and their moms and dads lift weights for fun and fitness, therapy and diversion. Can't watch *CNN* for a day without seeing a gym full of men and women pressing on as the newsperson cites research commending weightlifting for kids, the aging, the arthritic, the overweight, the underweight, the depressed, the pregnant, the diabetic.

The once-obscure, male-dominated peculiarity that raised eyebrows is now practiced by everybody in glittering gyms stretching sometimes over 50,000 square feet atop high rises in the big cities. We've become a mob.

In our quest, we made things far too complicated. Look, there are no secrets. You simply have basic God-given genetics, body chemistry and bone structure. And, provided the attributes of discipline and determination, you apply yourself full bore, and your body potential emerges, slow and sure.

THE SOAP OPERA

A person can arrive at a place and not be entirely sure how he got there. This place? The Brooklyn Academy of Music, a gothic structure composed of tall shadows, massive gray stone steps, arches, columns and pigeon-crowned portals.

It was tightly pressed into a space among towering angular buildings, mortar and concrete that had hardened at the turn of the century. The elegance of its gilded and velvet-curtained opera boxes was not lost on me, but the center of my attention stayed focused on the dark and dusty backstage closures, the grandness of which was expressed in bewildering height, intricate pulley and cable systems that raised, lowered and controlled vast curtains, backdrops, scenery and props, microphones, lights and speakers.

There, where the strings of the Philharmonic once rejoiced and Caruso pleaded, wept and conquered, I found a corner to drop my gym bag and prepare an ad-lib strategy for the unknown reckoning ahead: the Mr. America Contest, September, 1965.

I wasn't alone. Tough union stagehands, an amateur crew of fledgling assistants and volunteers, a team of Roloflex photographers and a splat of magazine and newspaper writers spilled over the stage and flowed into the theater's front rows as the judges congregated, shared war stories and sharpened their pencils. Pre-judging would start without fanfare when all the contestants seemed to be present.

The contestants, primed, ragtag and mighty—Mr. America and Mr. Universe lookalikes, dressed funny and still a little wet behind the ears. They were a new breed, putting on Man Tan and pumping up with The Samson Twister and Kool-aid.

Me? I don't mingle much and I mingled even less then. There was a strong showing from the Islands (Puerto Rico, Trinidad, Tobago and Jamaica) and they were jolly good. We laughed and had fun, and I'll never forget them. It was a time I didn't think I'd laugh—ever.

I took the long way to get to New York; I left New Jersey in the spring of 1963, stopped off in Los Angeles for a couple of years and arrived in New York in the fall of '65. It gave me a chance to think and see the sights. They've got sunshine out west.

You make friends when you're under stress and wearing the same witless outfit. And then there's the ritual of oil application done with machismo and very particular care. "Pumping up" presents no problem except for the sliding around and the overtraining, dehydration and hypoglycemia.

The dapper fellow who brought bananas, tuna and a water bottle knew what he was doing. He was the only guy who wore slippers, had a towel ever ready and didn't look like he'd been rolled in the back alley. He even had spray deodorant in his giant gym bag.

Pre-judging was a mass of confusion which suited me just fine. The more distracted everyone became, the easier it was to relax and observe. The immediate challenge was carbing up before the evening show: no carbs, no energy, no pump, no fun. For that, I joined Freddy Ortiz and his entourage at an authentic New York delicatessen, the original fast food of the Big Apple.

At one point, crazy Freddy removed his shirt in the middle of an intersection and stopped traffic as I ate a roast beef sandwich and drank a container of milk. He was warming up the crowd for the night's performance.

I envied his brashness. It took a net to get me onstage and hooks to pull off my clothes.

Pretty soon, Earl Maynard had his shirt off and was trying to pull down Freddy's pants. I was howling, down to a tank top and hitting double over-head biceps shots before a cheering yet ever-flowing stream of busy citizenry.

It must have been the carbohydrates or the relief that accompanies a sense of insignificance: Standing at the foot of skyscrapers among millions of souls is liberating.

As the evening progressed, Larry Scott and I stuck together behind the thick and impenetrable curtain. He knew the ropes—he'd been here before. You might say Larry had already ascended the heights of the famed landmark and returned to reminisce—The Dungeon of Santa Monica meets Vince's Gym of North Hollywood. There's gonna' be a party tonight.

Nothing that takes place backstage can compare to what goes on in a New York City audience, especially a bodybuilding audience, especially in 1965. The enthusiasm arrives in carloads, empties from subway stations, buses and taxicabs. Guys with wives and dudes with chicks on Saturday night and they are looking cool and feeling no pain.

But, wait, my friend. It's beyond that; there's something more and you can taste it. There's a tremor, a stir of expectation, a charge in the air, on the street and in the bowels of the elegant auditorium. It's not frightening; yet, it's not exactly without fright. It's an unknown, a mysterious, penetrating feeling.

Activity becomes more of a blur as the night goes on. I pump up again and again, smear more oil around, tire of nakedness, conversation and my now-greasy hairstyle gone mad. Smudged, fat and skinny at once, with nothing more constructive to do, I turn toward the throb of the night, the electricity of the squeals and the quake of the uproar.

The audience hasn't missed a beat. They like the dark rippling men from the Islands of the Caribbean. They like the spiffy homeboys and the thick Europeans.

Freddy poses in slow motion and shakes the century-old halls of grandeur; he tears down the house as he flexes his biceps and spreads his lats. This audience has not seen this stuff before tonight.

I stood behind Larry, Mr. California and the reigning Mr. America, as he edged toward the center dais. Excitement was building as the show neared its final moments. He was about to be introduced as the overwhelming winner of the Mr. Universe title...and pass the Mr. A. on to me.

The backstage grew soundless, the stony veteran stagehands whispering now, as if in suspense. Contestants froze in a line. An unnerving silence possessed the crowd, a restless stillness that gripped everyone at once; no one moved, as if waiting for a heartbeat. Larry stepped closer to the spotlight and paused as a silent, motionless silhouette.

The hush ached in our bones and tightened our jaws. Moving another step, he loomed forward, raising his massive arms overhead, along with the first and last note of music.

The sound that broke from the crowd was chilling. It was as if from one deep place a long contained emotion was released...a rolling thunder never before expressed in this tarnished and fading opera house; the chorus built upon itself, stunning its maker, an awesome rumble that stopped the heart.

I joined Larry to receive my trophy, the loving-child embrace of the Big City crowd. The spotlight, the applause, the center-stage dais were mine for long, fiery moments like the continuous striking of stick matches, suddenly ablaze, hissing, smoking and gone. Another, followed by another, then gone.

As I ponder the memories of that time, were I given the opportunity to repeat things, I would, glaring mistakes and all. The urge to edit out a few embarrassments and hurts exists, but who am I to tamper with history? As it is, so let it be.

If I'm proud, it's because I'm a muscle-building original. I invented, improvised and rooted about, along with a small, disconnected band of rebels with a cause: to build solid muscle and might through the austere, hard labor of love—the lifting of iron. Our shirts were not torn to be fashionable; they were shredded by use and outgrowth.

We didn't imitate. Who would be the model before us?

NICE WORK IF YOU CAN GET IT

Hollywood isn't just around the corner. It's a convoluted place where "stars" are born and celebrities of film and television work, congregate, celebrate, live n' play. Hollywood is famous and infamous, a stretch of boulevards that sparkle at night and attract the weirdest creatures known to man. It is alluring hillsides, scrappy and steep, upon which stilted houses perch and shaded hideaways snuggle. Privacy, secrecy, mystery and the unknown reside as an odd family in need of no one but each other.

I had seen a half-dozen movies and watched less than 50 fidgety hours of TV before I left the swampy shores of Secaucus for the emerald and gold of Santa Monica. I was clueless, penniless, green as unpicked apples...and dumb. I was also quiet, and in my silence people thought I was, perhaps, cool. Wrong, but it got me through the first months during which time I grew wider, and like a chameleon took on the colors of my surroundings.

I discovered something soon after my Muscle Beach arrival: acceptance and indoctrination.

Nobody worked. Wes, the lovable gym keeper, responsibly delivered mail for the postal service. Mighty Merle was a manager at Sears, and Ronnie "Lead-us" taught geometry at Venice High. The rest of the guys were dutiful members of the Screen Extras Guild. Their chosen profession required that they call the SEG hotline late each morning to inquire of possible "extras" work for the following day.

"Extras" work constituted the presence of any background person needed to complete a scene being filmed for either motion picture or television. You know the role—the soldier on the battlefield, the audience at the opera, or the man and lady chatting on the street corner. If work prevails, they spend the day on the set playing cards and gabbing until their services are needed. This activity provided a neat day's pay, and life was good.

On an outstanding day they picked up a bit part, which called for some action or speaking. "When the Captain arrives on the scene, get out of the police car and hand him the gun. Say to him, 'I found it in the bushes, Sir.'" Heightened the fun and the wage considerably.

Lights, camera, action.

Bad days meant no work and they filed for unemployment and hung out at the beach and lifted weights. Some guys hung out the whole summer when filming typically slowed to a crawl. Nice work if you can get it.

These guys and gals had a trim network going, and when work was coming up in the future, they were tuned in. The prosperous seasons were a gift from heaven; an ongoing extra part on a TV series was diamond-studded and came only to the honored, privileged and blessed.

Everybody I knew was a soldier on the 1960s favorite, *Combat.*

I think Zabo was a chief, my training partner was a spy, and a few big blond dudes were Kraut officers. I thought they had substantial occupations, Hollywood and all, and hoped I'd visit the place, and Disneyland, too, one day.

Can't do everything at once. I gotta get huge. I gotta get a car.

Anyway, one ordinary day, word circulated that the popular Los Angeles television station KHJ on Melrose in Hollywood was looking for a character to play the host of their upcoming Saturday prime-time evening show. The producers purchased a year's supply of male-hero films from the past—Victor Mature, Errol Flynn, Steve Reeves, those guys—and needed someone to introduce the flicks and visit with the audience during breaks throughout the presentation.

What ensued was a common Hollywood peculiarity—a cattle call—where everyone who in any way resembled the sought-after player shows up in flip flops and jeans, carrying lunch in a paper bag. One by one, they're sorted by an assistant and his assistant until only a handful remain.

I couldn't resist joining in the action.

When I got there, I noticed Vince Gironda sitting on a curb in front of the studio drinking a cup of coffee. He was called before the camera for a screen test while I milled around with the remaining short list like a stray dog. Is that Reg Lewis over there with Ray Rutledge and Dick Sweet, my training partner?

My name was announced and I was ushered onto a sound stage, placed before a marker and asked to read a handheld teleprompter that said, "Good evening, ladies and gentlemen, boys and girls, and you muscle worshippers. Welcome to *The Gladiator*. Tonight men with swords and shields will capture your hearts."

It must have been my Joisey accent. You ever hear a frightened bodybuilder from Secaucus pronounce "girls" or "worshippers"? He drops the Rs and kicks 'em around da flaw. I got the part and they called the show "*David, the Gladiator*."

Highest Saturday night ratings. I got a car.

UNDER THE PIER

1966, the year I won Mr. Universe, Larry Scott won the newly created Mr. Olympia title. We stood onstage together before the greatest-ever NYC audience. I was thrilled. My statement in bodybuilding was serendipitously and solidly made.

For me, the desire or need to enter or win Mr. Olympia didn't exist. Never did. I really just liked working out for a hundred other reasons. Though it was expected that I continue the competitive climb, I considered that striving accomplished. The enthusiasm for further title pursuits ceased that night.

From the earliest day, I trained to build muscle and might. It was as the crazy '60s lengthened that bodybuilding (not my favorite reference) took on critical mass and an acute change of direction. The control gates failed and the flood was sudden.

Posing took on unusual, self-centered proportions. A wardrobe of posing trunks, a library of posing music, posing skin creams and coloring lotions, negotiations to endorse products and conversations crowded with pump...and flex deflated the muscle building I loved.

It became a business. It became a scene; exit the Bomber.

I ignored the expanding bodybuilding world, not by rude intention, but it simply didn't interest me. It appeared to grow tentacles and I found it alien to my perception of muscle and might.

I dug the metal: the single-mindedness, the struggle, the intense body feelings, the pump and burn and heat and sweat. The battle, defeat, and mostly the victory, the wordless communication and knowing amid a very small tribe and, early on, the muddled or vacant stares I captured from puzzled, stumbling on-lookers—the rest of the world, really.

I don't think of it so much an ego trip, as being an amused ape comfortably aware of itself. Muscles for display was to me irrational, the peak of vanity, a frightening conceit. Instead, I liked to use that power and mass to overcome. Apply the strength gained for practical purpose; better yet, to build and create.

Once I got to southern California, I picked up on the '60s drift and began building oversized furniture out of pier wood to pay the mortgage. We ate, but spent no long weekends in the South of France with the jet set. Hard physical work appealed to me (loved it) and was a habit since my childhood years when delivering heavy boxes of groceries to the tenants of Hoboken, New Jersey.

One dismal day, I needed wood to build a one-of-a-kind bedroom set. The day was almost rainy, perfect for working under the moist and muffled pier. The structure was hundreds of yards by hundreds of yards, a vast aged wood and rusting metal emporium. Once a grand and popular amusement park, in the mid-70s the Pacific Ocean Park was deserted and scheduled for dismantling. It housed staggering vagrants sharing wine and mattresses in one or two dark pockets, and the remainder was mine. I kept to the shadows.

Equipped with my battered handsaw, I began to wander around the magnificent underside of the POP. Everything I needed was there in abundance, including the echoing rhythm of the surf, the salty wet air and a distinct sense of awareness that tingled with fear. It was dark, crisscrossed with timber bracing, illusionary, maze-like and off limits. Once I tripped over a body; another time I was followed to its depths by a pair of hairy muscular legs—stories for later, if I remember to tell them.

After carefully selecting each piece of pier wood, I gathered it in a pile at the pier's edge. No easy task, 5x7s and 3x12s—12 feet long, wet and slippery—cut, dragged, stacked and guarded...all after a tough early morning workout.

Across the sand 200 yards away sat my beat-up station wagon, built for the task. I sat atop the aging Douglas fir and assessed my treasure. One day soon, this stack would become a massive four-poster bed, two tables to match and a chest of drawers, burned, distressed and finely smoothed. Brass, leather and rusty metal would be affixed for a not-so-subtle touch. It would be cut, fitted, carved, drilled, bolted, pushed and pulled and turned over and over again until, with all its mistakes, it was just right.

Hungry, thirsty and getting chilly as the last of the year's sun went down, I prepared for the hardest part of the day, hauling my booty to the wagon. You see, it's all a workout. Reps counted while cutting off the planks. Sets counted as they're lugged, sorted and piled.

And now, the intense powerlifting match and strongman carry across the deep sand. Technique: Lean planks at a 45-degree angle against a piling, largest board on the bottom and stacked with sure balance.

Now, as if squatting or deadlifting, approach the pulpy weight, tight bodied, with focus, accomplishment and psychological might. By feel and instinct, locate the center of gravity with your strongest shoulder. Three deep breaths...LIFT...steady...one step at a time.

Another and another until the feat is done. That's how we do it.

I'M THE BOMBER

The clothes you wear on global crossings become like pajamas shortly after dinner and everyone on board gets as comfortable as possible… and very forgiving. Wrinkles are in and spots, stains and vague odors go unnoticed. You wallow until the captain announces that arrival is in two hours. The flight's last leg is devoted to restoration and renewal as enlivened passengers break out their slick disembarkation finery.

"I'm sorry, sir, but there were no trousers with your jacket. They must have fallen off the rack when we changed the craft in Hawaii," explained the attendant in a cute Aussie accent. I stared at her with my mouth open, failing to see the humor in the untimely joke. No joke?

I looked down and stared in disbelief. I was wearing a sweatshirt cut off at the elbows: more room to stretch and be piggy. The hideous gold broad-corduroy pants cinched around my waist fit when I weighed 250, but now resembled a potato sack partially filled with potatoes. Is this depression I feel or is it lack of sleep, low carbs, decompression disease or jet lag?

I was the last to descend the great aircraft stairway.

The press, garlands of flowers, pretty beauty queens in swimsuits and high heels were on hand to greet the spiffy Mr. America…on-the-spot daytime TV coverage. I tried to go out the rear of the craft with the trash and empty food bins, but security caught me pushing a dolly without a proper name tag. I can beg. Please. I just want to help… saurie, mayte.

I did my rotten best and made some friends in spite of myself. Paul Graham, the kind-hearted, street-wise Australian promoter put his thick arm around my shoulders and said, "We can do this, my man.

Relax; go to the hotel. I'll pick up your luggage and have it sent to your room. Two pieces, is it?"

I apologized to my new friends and planned to meet them in the morning for a workout.

My room was a suite high above the harbor overlooking the Opera House. Where I was and what I was doing settled in as I gazed at the grand sight. Eat, unwind, unleash. No exercise for two days made me antsy. I kicked up into handstand pushups to pump and burn the delts. Feels good, nothing like it.

Coming down from my third set, having already ordered a steak from room service, I kicked an oversized end table with a smash, breaking a lamp…and my foot. I'm beginning to look like a bloody fool.

Somehow you get through the mess called life and move onto the next mess. I didn't see my luggage for three days. Bugger.

"We think it's in Honolulu, sir, with your pants."

Australians are great. They didn't throw me to the crocs.

Morning appeared and I reluctantly got up and hobbled to the window. Thoughts of disaster evaporated as I watched the rising sun decorate the waterways and high rises with sparkling diamonds and shimmering gold.

The right foot was jammed, busted and swollen, but repair would come only with time, the friendly doctor assured me. No setting, no cast, no charge. These little white pills will get you through the weekend.

A knock at the door was followed by Paul, his mates—now mine—and breakfast.

"After food, we'll get you some clothes and hit the uptown gym for a workout. Whattaya say, mate?"

While in another hemisphere and training in an unfamiliar gym, I was content to accept anything that resembled a workout; I was content to accept no workout at all. I have, under the best of conditions, a few minor discomforts to negotiate when training in a strange gym: self-consciousness, privacy, workout effectiveness and…um…ego.

What if they recognize me and I have to maintain an image? (I thought he was taller, younger, bigger and stronger.)

Worse yet, what if they don't recognize me? Hi, I'm The Bomber. The what? I'm the original Blond Bomber and I've been blasting the gyms around the world. Proud of it and I'm famous, too. Don't let the foot fool you.

Can you imagine the misunderstandings and explanations just trying to get a pump? Search, hand cuff, interrogate…

I got past the front counter and stood at the edge of a comfortable, well-equipped, energetic and packed gym. Just the right size work area with all the tools, only there were people everywhere; some sort of weekend celebration had them all amped up. They weaved between the machines and gathered by the squat racks and water fountain. I spied a bench about to be vacated and casually limped to it, snagging a pair of matching 25s along the way; they were light, but they were there.

The point now was to keep moving so no one asked to work in or borrow my puny-yet-precious dumbbells. Sitting on the end of the bench and looking downward to avoid eye contact, I scanned the scene to get my bearings, the dumbbells hanging by my side.

A 12-inch block lay near a column three feet to my left. I needed it to raise my bench and add some originality to the beginnings of what appeared to be a feeble workout.

How do I get the block without leaving my post? I want that block.

I assumed a mildly transfixed expression and did a seated variation of rolling shoulder shrugs to warm up and position myself advantageously in the direction of the block. It had a cutout on the side that served as a handle. Shrugs completed, I placed the 25s on the floor and rolled them to within inches of the block, very carefully arranged my sore foot on the bench and proceeded to do a set of medium-grip pushups, dumbbells still in hand.

On the last rep I released my left-hand grip and snatched the block like a lizard snatching an insect for dinner. I uprighted myself and planted the block under one end of the bench as if it had been forever attached.

Now we're ready to blast.

Blasting with 25-pounders requires some improvising. I laid back on the incline, put my feet up on the bench and lowered the dumbbells toward the floor. From that position with my palms forward, I raised the weights in a curling movement, a tight contraction at the chest and shoulders and a slow full extension down, pause, and back up. A set of 10, and I press the dumbbells overhead, palms facing each other, to starting position number two. From the overhead position, I lowered both weights with concentration in a perfect triceps extension movement to burn and pump the back of the arms; 10 reps and mission accomplished.

I slightly rearrange my extended arms, allowing them to reach back and outward as I lower the weights in a fly movement to affect the pecs and lats at once. This action is difficult and done precisely, with a three-count pause at its peak of extension, followed by a slow return, pause, and continuation for another 10 reps.

The timing is right to sit up, shift to the end of the bench, bend forward and allow the no-longer-puny 25s to hang to the floor. My legs are together and I'm resting my torso on the thighs. The breaths are coming on strong and the pump is solidifying.

The burn is being chased around the upper body like a scalded hound dog. I'm in heaven. I tug the dumbbells from a palm-counterpoised placement into a rear deltoid-slash-back movement and knock out 10 mean reps.

I sit up calmly and place the weights on my thighs as I review the room that was lost to me for the past five minutes. It's looking a whole lot better after a pump, a burn and some sweat. I shake my hands one by one as I resume my easy breathing. The dumbbell rack is still bare except for some cute pink things nobody'll go near. Fine by me. I've got my hands full. I start the process again: shrugs, curls, extensions, flys, bent-over laterals. A total of five delirious sets with minor pauses for minor adjustments, and it's time to move on.

Is that an 80-pounder that young man is about to unloose? If I coordinate this move just right, I can replace the 25s, descend upon the big thing and drag it over here before the crowd notices. Done.

Heavy compared to the 25s, I prepare to do one-arm dumbbell rows for some full back work. Knee up on the bench is not my style, but by employing the technique, I retain possession of the surface, as I require it for the stiff-arm pullovers that will follow in my favorite superset fashion. Five sets of six to eight reps. I'm all smiles.

Excuse me; are you finished with the 80? Oh, yeah. Sure, pal. Help yourself.

I lie back on the bench, feet up, and knock out 25 slow contractions followed by 25 leg raises followed by 25 tucks off the end of the bench. Ten minutes of this act and I am done.

The bench is bolted to the floor. I decide to leave it.

DUNGEON DUTY

I set out from my home, an apartment on Copeland Court in Santa Monica, fueled with my 1960s standard pre-workout meal, two rounded tablespoons of defatted and desiccated beef-gland powder and eight ounces of water. It mixed, sort of, and went down the throat like everyday dirt. Mud in a tumbler was a ritual I practiced stoically every morning, a sacrifice to the gods of iron and steel. Endurance and rock-hard muscle is what I sought. Mr. America was behind me and the Universe ahead. Whatever it took.

The streets were quiet in the early morning, as usual—traffic those long years ago not up to the density and madness of today. I was driving a fire-engine-red Corvette with the top down and the hood of my sweatshirt up. The nip of California fall was in the air. My mind was in limbo as the car rumbled toward the Muscle Beach gym, the tabernacle and the altar.

There was something in the air, a mystery, I could feel it and I didn't know what it was; I didn't want to know and I didn't look. It would reveal itself, I was sure. It always did.

Funny thing, I don't ever recall questioning when I was bound for the gym why I was bound for the gym. Never was there room for a wedge to be placed that might separate me from my workout. No mission to accomplish drove me onward, no definitive goal, no exact target, no tangible end result. Weight lifting and building muscle and strength largely and simply defined my life. I worked, worked out, struggled to pay my bills, slept and ate, laughed and cried. I was still a child of the east coast and there ain't nuttin' wrong with that.

No searching for a parking space, I pulled directly in front of the Dungeon's entrance, a pair of faded poster- and graffiti-covered doors hanging crookedly on rusty hinges. They appeared locked, but I had the key—lift up firmly on handle and pull vigorously, place rock against door to keep open.

No alarm sounded. I was in.

That I was in was not a thrill. It was necessary, it had to be, it was a must, the unspoken rule of my life; now to find my way to the switch box to throw some light on the scene. Throwing some light was not unlike striking a match and lighting a pair of votive candles. I come, I see, I do. Let's get to work.

Everything was there, just as the day before. I saw tired Olympic bars, multitudes of scattered plates like families of turtles heading for the sea, and hulking dumbbells stretched out on sagging wooden racks. The dumbbells reminded me of hoods I knew in Jersey who took numbers and worked for the unions, a gnarly and troublesome bunch if you didn't know them.

What was in the corners darkened by the night, under the hidden stairwell and in that back room where junk was stored and no one goes, I didn't care or wonder. Big spiders and rats, I expected.

Situps, leg raises and hyperextensions intended to strengthen my midsection, gave me comfort in the shadowy stillness. I forced my energy and deep breathing into the dead space, resuscitating it as if it were a languishing ghost. Soon we were both warm bodies and alive. The dried animal glandulars—and youth and determination—were kicking in.

Nobody interrupted the early morning solitude—just the way I liked it, bleak and harsh in the subterranean confines contrasting with the warmth and light at the top of the long narrow staircase. At the far end of the gym, the lifting platform beneath the sidewalk skylights beckoned me with a lonely call. The mystery of the early morning was beginning to unfold.

I plodded over like a young bull coaxed by mild tugs on his nose ring, a curious and innocent beast sensing a mate waiting in the brush.

This bull was weighing 245 pounds and eating lots of protein. I did a set of bench presses, as one does to penetrate the cold, wet waters; the plates clanged loudly. The tranquility was broken. Every cracked wall and dank corner bristled with the reverberations. An unconscious shudder announcing "we've begun" went through my body. It's time. Lift with all your might until it's over.

I stood on the warped lifting platform, its original geometric flatness rearranged by time, moisture and the thunder of the weights dropping furiously from overhead year after year. I loaded the straightest bar I could find in the creeping morning light. There it lay, an Olympic bar and a 45-pounder—a wheel—on each side, 135 pounds.

I did a second set of benches to continue my warm-up. Felt good, real good. Revisiting the platform, I stood over the handsome construction and rolled it forward and back with my foot. Impulsively I bent over, grasped the weight, pulled it to my shoulders and pressed it overhead for reps. I was testing the small mass, kicking tires, squeezing melons at the market. Felt good, real good.

Sitting again at the bench press, I felt my gaze return to the platform. Irresistible. The bench press suddenly seemed one dimensional compared to the overhead press—incomplete, less engaging, not as expressive or interesting. The standing press was tougher and more critical. I found myself adding another wheel to each side. It was Monday, not my favorite day, but I was fresh.

I cleaned the 225, pressed it for two reps and returned it to its place on the hard rubber mats. Delightful.

I'd done bentover rows seriously, heavy reverse curls regularly, and my benches weren't bad, but I wasn't real familiar with overhead pressing. You might say this was the beginning.

I was now circling the gym floor with my belt in hand, searching for chalk. In the Dungeon, chalk was stashed out of sight by the hardcore who liked the white-powder ritual and needed the gripping advantage. I slid a 25 on each side, made the appropriate clang and locked the weight in place with thick collars. I squinted at the pile like it was trouble and resumed my hunt.

The floor was still empty, gray had replaced the blackness and I was hot with sweat and cold with its evaporation.

I confronted the well-balanced and thickening heap of iron with respect, my attitude taking on the gravity of the weight before me. The objective was to move the weight to my shoulders in one sudden surge of power, make some quick and sure adjustments and press the mass steadily overhead until my arms were locked and torso stable and upright—hold it for a couple seconds and return it to the platform sensibly.

I'd practiced this procedure half a dozen times earlier in the spring with less weight and less intensity. No problem. I was younger then and it was less important than now.

Deep breath, grasp, clean and press. Job done well with arms reaching and the weight close to the sky. I hear the sound of life in the distance, a figure doing chins a mile away. The day has begun.

I know what I have to do. Off comes the quarter and on goes another 45.

The plates made tight with a rumble one side at a time, the heavy collars are locked in place and the bar is brushed with chalk. I tug on the mass for good measure and turn to the process of preparing and psyching for the battle: belt, pacing, standing, considering and chalking.

Self consciousness is fought, doubt is beaten off, extraneous thoughts are eliminated and energy is focused. These the toughest aspects of the battle. Seeking a culmination of all that is positive and enthusiastic and good and right, I bend over to do it again.

This, the lifting of an impossible weight on a bar, is not something we repeat. Each time is the first time, if it is any good. The procedures have a sameness and continuity about them—position the body, bend, grasp, clean, press and return—but the fury between each step is always new, spontaneous and redefining.

Man against steel, steel against man, man against himself. We've got our hands full, crew.

Up it went with back-breaking fullness. I staggered briefly after the clean, my legs remained locked as I pressed and, yes, I leaned like an oak in high winds, but I did not stall or jerk or otherwise falter. I stood and reached and reached and stood for blinding seconds before lowering the weight, letting it go a foot from its resting place.

When you're alone after remarkable success, satisfaction and gratefulness whirl in your mind with no place to go. They were self-contained, while colorful flashes and mad sounds of rushing filled my head and a wonderful ache flooded my pulsating body.

I did it, I whispered with an insufficient shrug: recuperate, oxygenize. I was leaning on my arms, breathing smoothly and staring at my recently acquired friend, 315 pounds of steel, when someone called out from the center of the gym floor.

I turned and there's Jack Hughes, a wiry lifter from a generation gone by who was then a coach and judge of powerlifting and Olympic lifting contests on the coast. "Good lift, Draper," he said, "Don't see too many guys pressing 325 at 7 o'clock on a Monday morning."

I thanked him without pretension, being a very young member of a very old club. I also said I had 315 pounds on the bar. He pointed out I had 325 on the bar and hadn't accounted for the 10 pounds of lock-tight collars. He left, and I did it again.

True stories don't grow on trees. Today I couldn't roll 325 pounds across the floor even if I succeeded loading it on a bar in the first place. That doesn't make me a bum.

Once a bomber, always a bomber.

MGM TOWN

The cattle call that served to locate Harry Hollard of *Don't Make Waves* was not unlike the prior *Gladiator* scenario. The word flooded the gyms like Gatorade, and muscular actors buoyed to the surface. This time, the setting was the famous MGM Studios in Culver City, where silent films were made and Gable, Bogart and Monroe applied makeup, lunched and shouted, whispered and winked into the polished lenses.

The privilege was monumental—to enter the hallowed halls of the marvelously rundown studios that echoed of stardom and celebrity. No tourist could buy a ticket to this show.

The hopefuls lined up to register their names in a less-than-orderly fashion. The distracted guards unwittingly gave me the opportunity to wander down the driveways between the massive studio walls, peer at their heights and pretend to be a part of their importance.

I noted the blinking red warning lights at entry ways that indicated filming was under way: Silence, please...do not enter. The great and unseen powers were at work piecing together another lifetime full of wonders and more emotions than those we knew as our own—heroes and heroines more alive than the people with whom we worked, ate and slept.

I couldn't help but feel lost, ordinary and alone. Jealous is ugly.

I moved on, hastening across an abandoned and dusty street front with wooden walkways, hitching posts and wooden wagons in front of old clapboard storefronts and a sheriff's office. Confused for a second, I hesitated and glanced to the left and the right; long early morning shadows still formed and a breeze stirred an embroidered curtain in an open window above the Mercantile.

The strong smell of coffee wafted along the street and I imagined it came from the saloon or the hotel on the corner. Small chirping birds circled overhead and flapped their way to a sprawling oak tree beyond a white fenced cottage. A sudden roar broke the calm and antiquity of the make-believe world. I spun to confront a diesel tractor-trailer bearing down Main Street with a plush mobile home in tow, "Director" written in bold letters above the front door.

I waved as they rumbled by, just another prop man or electrician earning a wage. A Boeing 727 appeared overhead in the near skies as it readied for landing at the Los Angeles International Airport a couple miles away. I grabbed the wooden and metal spokes of an old wagon wheel and tugged to stretch my lats and flex my grip.

The sound of a bullhorn in the distance seemed to be giving orders to dutiful wannabe actors—something about the next bus to backlot three.

With pause and reluctance, I returned to the group, wondering where I was going.

At one point, I was sitting on a vast green and grassy slope where the camera on a dolly and a boom mike were positioned. It was sunny, warm and casual. One by one, the performers who made the final cut were given their one-minute before the directors, producers and assorted attendants. We were requested to walk up the lawn hand in hand with a Sharon Tate look-alike to a mark five feet from the camera, face each other, speak clumsy sweet nothings, turn and walk away.

I thought for sure Larry Scott would get the part, as he was a confident and capable guy who already had worked in a *Beach Party* movie and was occasionally seen doing strings of cartwheels and back flips in good form across the manicured lawn. Mr. California, after all.

Hollywood is full of surprises. The greatest part about being chosen for a co-starring role in a feature film is being chosen.

The second part is working.

This ever happen to you? You recall incidents in your life when you were much younger and wish you could do them over, not to make major changes, but to tidy them up a bit? Born in the east coast vacuum, I was slow to appreciate the things that were happening to me in the brave new world.

Working side by side with Tony Curtis, who couldn't have been more impressive, generous, fun and easy, was a privilege diluted by my stunted self-esteem. Tony got through to me and easily revealed his own insecurity, which we all share, when his words before the camera would not come.

He stood with me off camera and said, "Sometimes I can remember my lines, but they vanish when the director calls for action. I step off the set, close my eyes and in the blackness of my mind, I'm able to relax and go back to work in 30 seconds. Don't worry, Dave. It happens to everybody."

He genuinely laughed when he tried to lift a "refrigerator" I'd been carrying around the set most of the day. The crew dared him to move it to the background—it didn't budge. He thought they'd nailed it to the floor to provoke his competitive nature, expecting him to move it or die. He called their bluff early on and I, on cue, walked over, grabbed it and carried it up a short flight of stairs. Between scenes slapstick.

The old refrigerator trick is always good for a few laughs. Just don't ask me to tell a joke.

Sharon Tate was younger than I and a few solid steps ahead. We became friends like kids do in school. I carried her books.

She was wrapped up with Roman Polanski and I was married. She felt unthreatened and we could pal around and travel together when promotions required our presence. One night, she held onto my arm and wouldn't let go as our four-passenger aircraft worked its way through a storm on a flight to Charlotte for a preview of *Don't Make Waves.*

Adventure in daily life.

THE YEAR WAS 1967

THE PLACE WAS MUSCLE BEACH

THE CONTEST WAS MR. BIG BOY

THE WINNER WAS HARRY HOLLARD

There was no segue between the contests and the acting. The two ventures occurred side by side, like running and jumping as a kid when life is a breeze.

During those early days, as was the tradition, I responded with all the other muscle guys in southern California to a Hollywood cattle call seeking a muscleman. As I've told you before, the major Los Angeles studio, KHJ-TV, chose me, for some unknown reason, to be *David, the Gladiator,* the host of the year-long presentation of Saturday night TV adventure movies.

I was a local celeb for a year, though I didn't know it at the time. Mr. America was busy training for Mr. Universe. It was amid that training that another cattle call echoed through the beaches and gyms in close proximity to Hollywood. Filmways of MGM needed one Harry Hollard to lift weights on Muscle Beach in *Don't Make Waves.* The bulk of the filming was completed in mid-September, the same week I competed in and won Mr. Universe, 1966.

It was all as if by accident and coincidence, as no ambition or planning is evident in either experience.

You have no idea how growing up in the swamplands of Secaucus in the '50s stunts one's growth and awareness. I pursued little more than the last rep and the next gram of protein.

I wasn't hustling Hollywood, knocking down doors or studying while I strived to become an actor.

I was super lucky—blessed by God, actually—to do what I did in Hollywood, and was between times of further good luck. European-hero filmmaking was momentarily spent and American hard-bodied stars were yet to be born and embraced during my blip on the screen.

There was another side door I passed through in movie making: *Lord Love a Duck.* A thought of Roddy McDowell is the first stirring memory that comes to my mind as I think of those days. For those weeks on the set and on location for my minor role in the movie, the two of us had neither met nor talked.

Then one hot afternoon, we concurrently entered an outdoor john placed discreetly behind the Santa Monica Courthouse, the scene of the day's filming. As we stood there in the stinking heat attending the most important business of the day, we talked about the weather, the ocean and the hard day's work. Nice guy.

We buttoned up, nodded, and I never saw him again.

I was in a fight scene in that movie. I vividly remember stepping into a dark, off-set area with a cameraman, a stunt man and a funky, rumpled bedroom mattress. The stunt man was 160 pounds and all business; I was 240 and curious about our brief and unspoken relationship. I was not welcomed, informed, consulted or directed. I was motioned. Fine.

Camera sez to Stunts, dragging the mattress, "This is a good spot."

Stunts drops the mattress, mutters something to me. I eagerly nod and next thing, I'm flying over his shoulder and onto the miserable mattress. I bounce like a fresh 240-pound sack of raw, living flesh on a mattress of lifeless straw.

Camera sez, "Got it," and Stunts sez, "Good."

I walked at a tilt for a week, looking for a pair of wise guys with a shabby mattress and a camera.

Another time, I did a guest spot on an amusing episode of *The Monkees* and was honored to work with the guys. I admired their young world of fame and celebrity and fun.

Though New Jersey was a few years behind me, I wasn't yet broken of my naiveté. (Alas, I never will be.) I stood on the sandy shores of a beach on a studio back lot, looked down on Davy Jones and, as the cameras rolled, said, "Beat it, twerp."

Davy flipped out.

The script called for the uncomplimentary designation "shrimp," not the "t" word, which evidently held an especially nasty connotation to Davy Jones of the Monkees.

He assumed a karate stance facing me, which called the action to a halt. Already nervous, out of my territory and getting hungry, my jaw dropped. It took me a full 10 seconds to realize the guy wanted revenge—and the crew around him, assistant director, wardrobe, makeup and stage hands were holding him back.

I was bewildered. I did something really wrong. Oh, geez.

Clusters of people gathered according to rank and job description. Where did I belong? I started to move toward a group of carpenters, when I was encompassed by a handful of fidgeting executives—where did they come from?—imploring me to apologize to the star.

I said absolutely, sure, no problem, certainly, you bet, guys. I was reluctant to ask why, but decided the information would help me in my sincerity and prevent me from stepping into another pile.

"Sorry I called you a twerp, Mr. Jones."

My apology was awkward, but I was sufficiently contrite. We went back to work and the sun shined on Burbank.

Those were short interludes (there were a few others), but the big Hollywood memory is certainly *Don't Make Waves.* Sandy McKendrick, the director, a nice man and an honor to know and work with, asked me to lunch at the MGM cafeteria early in production.

He was quiet and I was quiet, and from there on he would point and I would go.

He was looking for an image of a musclehead on screen and my incompetence as an actor portrayed that image rather well. I'd miss cues, look naturally unsure of myself, forget my lines and make up my own. Sandy must have thought, "Why screw it up? Just let him be himself."

Tony Curtis was a prince and Sharon Tate was not unlike a female version of me.

I liked Tony and felt equality with him, though I tended to kneel when he stood by my side. He was fun, honest and full of energy and I enjoyed my time with him.

Sharon was young and consumed by her attendees and guardians. She was a star in the making and I watched her from a distance. She was gutsy and willing and quiet and wanting to yell, I think.

One time I already told you about, we flew in a small aircraft over South Carolina and through that she held tightly onto my hand, yet she didn't hesitate to leap high from a trampoline and into my arms during filming. We hung in the shade and talked about this or that or nothing until it was our turn to tumble through that forsaken house in Malibu.

Off the set during breaks, like metal to a magnet, I chose to hang with the extras during lunch and the lengthy breaks. I was invited to eat at the long table with the lead actors and the director's crew and the production people, but I chickened out.

In reality, I felt it would be a disloyalty to my own—a snub, a dishonoring, false. I chose to relax among the few I knew. We lifted, sunned, had curling contests, did back flips in the sand, worked the trampoline, read, nodded and twitched and scratched.

A smarter person would have enjoyed the companionship of the cast and crew. They were terrific people, admirable and had a lot to offer a guy if he was half awake and not so darn shy and unsure of himself.

Don't Make Waves wasn't an accurate portrayal of the southern California bodybuilding scene, nor was it a mindless spoof. The early bodybuilding scene, like a diamond, had many facets. It was dumb and innocent and lazy, and it was fast, sharp and visited by courageous and hard-working men and women.

There were artists, mail carriers, airline pilots, cops, engineers, school teachers, heroes and bums. Some lived in the back of their cars or at the old Muscle House on the beach or in homes in Culver City and North Hollywood.

The picture was painted by one man's brush and palette of colors. Hollywood highlighted it with bright tones and impressionist strokes. Yeah, the picture's worth framing and hanging on a favorite wall in your living room. Better than another fading sunset or a still life of wilting flowers.

There were negatives in that filming memory: One sunny afternoon in the late summer, a small crowd of crew, actors and extras watched in fascination as parachutists descended a half-mile off Malibu Beach, the location depicting the famed Muscle Beach.

A daring team was shooting the skydiving sequence featured in *Don't Make Waves.* One chute fell quickly and there was alarm, fear. Small speed boats raced to the site, too late to rescue the cameraman who became entangled in the cords and sank into the sea. We all witnessed his death in cold, helpless disbelief.

Then, not long later, the set designer, a favorite character at the studios and on location, like Bo Jangles up and died one day. Where was the enthusiastic Italian inspiration with colorful fabrics draped over his arm, towing props and offering encouraging words with the lilt of a language no one could speak but everyone understood?

Gone in silence. Cancer, they said.

Rumors of a monster budget crunch added a gray cloud to the mostly sunny skies.

These were the incidents of life, the junk, the crap that happens here and there and everywhere and were not particular to *Don't Make Waves* or my involvement in the project. There were no negative experiences for me personally, unless I look back and see the things I would rather have done better.

The positives came on a daily basis. Being an actor and the familiar part of a Hollywood film production was subtly awesome. I could go here or there with freedom and permission. The guard at the studio gate waved me through…Hey, Dave…the prop man asked my advice; makeup fussed over my eyebrows; the director asked if I was ready before he said, "Rolling…and…action."

I won Mr. Universe during the last week of major filming and was awarded a hand-painted sketch by the MGM art department of an Oscar in a muscle pose, titled *Super Oscar for Mr. Universe.* It's enclosed in an antique gold frame made by the MGM prop department and says above the statuette, "We're Proud of You."The cast and crew signed it, and it now hangs on a wall above the staircase.

The filming led to 15 minutes on stage with Johnny Carson while he showed me off to his audience like a prize bull. How can you beat that?

There's usually no one reason we do or don't do important things in life; there's a list.

I was neither internally prepared, nor internally directed toward an acting career. In my life, stuff either happens or it doesn't. Pursuing the rocky road and crossing the barrens and climbing the heights was too much trouble for something without substance—a hope, a dream, a passion.

I took acting classes for two years with good young actors under a popular director, Peyton Price, but I didn't study acting. The artistic or egotistic or materialistic or fame and power-thirsty tentacles were either underdeveloped in me, or they had withered.

I quickly tired of interviews and cold readings and playing the necessary Hollywood games. I was between *Hercules Unchained* and *Rambo*—Reeves and Stallone—and was slightly out of step. There's more to the tale, but I had to leave town and head for the clear air of the Santa Cruz hills.

It was a priceless trip through the famed and curious streets of Hollywood where the action is: the secret and private alleys where the elite movers walk about, nonchalant and privileged; the off-limits studios, stages and backlots—workplaces of celebrities; the junky and crammed offices interviewing the sad wannabes for a one-time one-liner and the well-tanned, slick, gray-haired dude making a million-dollar deal as his Rolls unwinds the hills overlooking the town of tinsel.

Makes you want to laugh, cry, beg and steal.

Makes me smile to think about it.

ONCE UPON A TIME

Traveling back to 1966 is no short journey and as I begin to write, it seems I may have lost the way. I know this giant kid, Henrik Nielsen from Denmark or some faraway place, who yearns for the good old days. He calls upon me occasionally to summon up those years in the mid-60s when muscle building was like a grand piano with stout, carved wooden legs, ivory keys, gold inlay and rich, magical tones—no slick, assembly-line plastic cabinet with spun-chrome dials, synthesizers and massive Dolby Sound System to project exaggerated music. He missed what he and a lot of folks refer to as "The Golden Era of Bodybuilding."

A popular writer of the days gone by tells us the days were "real, undiluted and raw; the un-torched first growth—pure."

Put the filter of time on a moment, a day or an era, add slow motion plus your favorite sounds, apply shades of black and white with brilliant color, and it's all legendary, pulsing and dramatic. Nostalgia is more precious than the present, more real, friendlier and informative. Today will be more important tomorrow…next year.

I know all about the '60s; I believe I was there. Henrik is a kid like you and me, a kid at heart who wants to know what the lifting scene was like back when I trained for the Mr. Universe Contest. I should have taken notes; it was a very busy year.

The year before, I won Mr. America in the same venue, the Brooklyn Academy of Music. As I recall, I was a lot younger in 1965 than I was in '66. Living in California—my third year since migrating from the east coast—accelerated my growth like a shot of hormones.

My lifelong friendship with the Muscle Beach peculios (nonconformists) deepened and I became engaged in the casting and eventual filming of

Don't Make Waves. Working in Hollywood with hollyweird people and training in The Dungeon with a bunch of bulging guys smelling of DMSO tilted and stretched my already contorted east coast persona.

Oddly, my training didn't change from the prior year and my nutritional walk followed the same sound path. I had stumbled into what worked for me; I discovered a vein of gold and just kept digging. At 23, I realized that working the basics hard and consistently was the direct route to reaching my potential.

Granting myself a quarter for experimentation and variation and bulking up on high-protein, low-sugar food for six months in the fall and winter provided the stress-free anabolic environment we all need to grow: lots of first-class muscle-building, power food with no dieting struggle, lots of hard work with both feet on the ground rather than on a high-tension tight rope, no close and worrisome critical analysis, room for mushrooming buoyancy and faith.

And grow I did, not like a weed, but slowly and surely.

What I say here is important to the wandering musclebuilder who is ever-seeking the perfect and right routine. Settled on my training scheme, confident and determined, I worked and worked, without doubt and without vacillation. I didn't harass or plague myself with growth-inhibiting and time-wasting fear that I would not improve.

The 25-percent training margin reserved for adjustment and spontaneity allowed me to think on my feet and maintain a sense of freedom in my labor of love.

The folly of questioning my system would not numb my spirit and enthusiasm. I pressed on.

In the early spring of '66, a casting call echoed through the then-sparse muscle-building communities of southern California and a small herd of Popeyes and Tarzans made their way to the Hollywood studio. I was eventually cast as Harry Hollard in the film version of Muscle Beach, *Don't Make Waves,* and two weeks later I stood on a hillside in Malibu Canyon weighing 245 pounds beside Tony Curtis weighing much less. Filming had begun.

In early scenes—May of '66—my cohorts, Reg Lewis and Chet Yorton and I trundled about on-camera in our off-season bulkiness. Filming had me up at 5:00 am for an early morning one-hour blast at the gym, at make-up by 6:30 and on the set in the MGM studio at 7:00 or on location in Malibu at 8:00.

The days with the crew and actors around the lights, camera and action were fascinating and privileged and tantalizing; even the behind-the-scenes boredom was exciting, Hollywood picture-making tedium. I basked. When the day ended, it was back to the Dungeon for some serious lifting, which became more serious as the filming ended, and the Mr. Universe contest coincidentally neared. Mid-September was a blur of events.

The sun shined brightly through the summer and not every day was a workday, nor was any day tough: "Sit, stand, speak and roll over... once again, people, and...cut...that's a take."

Contest training didn't suffer and I ate mightily from my trusty Igloo. My commonness clung to me like wet underwear. Where the elite actors ate with aplomb from a daily catered banquet, I joined the rascals from Muscle Beach who comprised the extras, rapscallions playing poker in the shade with quarters.

I didn't gamble; I didn't take chances. Sometimes we'd bench press or do standing barbell curls with our backs against a pole for singles. Lunching on iron and steel was a sure thing.

Throughout the summer and as the September date neared, I slowly dropped bodyweight—wild guess, a pound a week—aiming for 230. The heavy bodyweight gained in the winter gave me freedom and power to roam and kept my mind off the corralled details:

veins, shape, definition and tone. Training and filming sufficiently distracted me, allowing the contest less priority and, therefore, less opportunity to defeat me.

One day, I woke up and it was Thursday; the studio cleared my plans and I was on my way to the airport heading east. Saturday was the Miss Americana, Mr. America, Mr. Universe and the second annual Mr. Olympia contests in The Brooklyn Opera House. I'd been there before in a former life.

I can't say my homework paid off. I did what I did the year before, only a little better, with more finesse and less numbness. I trained, ate, slept and worked and played. I wasn't sure I was going to win, I wasn't sure I was going to lose—I was sure I was going to show up on time.

The whole affair was less daunting than 1965. I held my breath for shorter periods of time and the win was as grand, though I can't recall the details as I do with my first extraordinary experience.

The audience was thicker than a jungle and, like a jungle heaved with wildlife, screamed and leaped, squealed and snarled with ferocious excitement. Larry Scott, thick and powerful as a Clydesdale, graciously accepted the Mr. Olympia crown (again), and said goodbye to competition.

Don Howorth, with his shoulders knocking over stagehands and microphones every time he turned left or right, won Mr. America.

I remember Miss Americana was…she…well, actually, I can't remember her at all. I have no doubt she was a beauty, but I must have been backstage pumping up, carbing up, oiling up, hiding… who knows? Bodies were everywhere.

The show ends in a triumphant blaze, emotions are emptied in a rush, the emcee, almost suddenly, bids "good night and farewell" in an optimistic tone, and it all stops.

The whole raucous, bountiful, resplendent extravaganza is unplugged.

The lights dim and the union stagehands unceremoniously gather wires, platforms, props and background curtains. The entrails of the wondrous event are exposed and discarded before the whooping spectators as they retreat from a memory under construction.

Restless and wired fans uncoil, food places fill up and the commotion backstage is subdued. The producers, judges and volunteers exchange stories and phone numbers, make plans for a late dinner and next year. It's 1:00 am. The competitors, the winners and losers, lick their wounds, drink the last of their water and wipe off patches of oil.

A rare, in-shape group that has expended all the energy of a small town tugs at its reserves to pull itself up and drag itself home. I'm amid the spent yet indefatigable group running on empty.

We all live somewhere far away. I have a flight back to LA in the morning. Shooting resumes at MGM Studios on Monday morning.

"Howorth. Larry. Let's grab a cab."

Ahda…Ahda…ahdat's all, folks.

GOOD GYMS ARE FROM HEAVEN

A gym is any place an athlete and the training apparatus meet: chinning and dipping bars in the basement, the track and field at a local high school, stairs and hills in the neighborhood, a punching bag hanging in the garage or a bar and a heap of dinged plates in the corner of a bedroom.

I started with the chins and dips at the tender age of eight and graduated without haste to the weights under the bed by my 10th year. As an authentic musclehead by the end of my teens, I pursued my master's degree through research and study at various muscle institutes across the globe. There were numerous gymnasiums of prominence, from New York to Rhodesia, and they served me well.

One does not pick up a weight in a gym in a back alley of central Madrid or Reg Park's smart fifth-floor health club in Johannesburg without learning something special. Choosing a pair of dumbbells from a rack in Vince's Gym with Don Howorth on your left and Larry Scott to your right does not leave you unchanged.

The lessons learned are often misplaced, but never lost; they're deeply and privately stored away, but not forgotten; their effects are always present in one's being, but not necessarily distinct and discernible.

However, some experiences are overpowering and they reappear frequently, giving indication of their profound influence in one's formation and education. I've created a list I call "Most Unforgettable Gyms" in an exercise to recall and relive the occasions that so stimulated me in the years gone by. I hope to stir up something old worth remembering.

Life constantly refreshes itself.

My first venture in weight training outside the confines of the bedroom gym (three such bar-under-the-bed arrangements from ages 10 to 19 years) was celebrated at the classic YMCA in Elizabeth, New Jersey.

The building was old in 1960, in an old part of the congested old town, and the gym was in the oldest part of the building, a room in the basement…next to the boiler. Where else? The room was shaped like an L with each intersecting protrusion the size of a bedroom. I was doomed, it seemed, to cramped bedroom-size training and feared I might not grow spacious, living-room-size muscles.

The area was packed with scattered weights, boards that served as benches and loud, robust dock workers. I was thrown into the den of madness by Joey Dinetta, the reigning Mr. New Jersey and my new buddy, who promised to show me the ropes. I'd never seen nor heard of Olympic bars or plates, nor had I witnessed more than one pair of dumbbells at one time in one place. Iron was everywhere, leaning, lying flat and moving fast up and down and left and right.

Once I got used to ducking or hitting my head on various low-slung water pipes and bumping into walls, bodies and equipment, I found myself responding to the energized social atmosphere, the big bars and the diversity of exercises. I learned, I grew and life was good.

After a season in the low-ceilinged subterranean twin cubicles in need of paint, light, ventilation and space, I headed for the city—Jersey City.

Vic Tanny was making his way around the country, gyms here and there, during the late 1950s and the early '60s. Right in the heart of Journal Square—Jersey City's miniature version of Times Square—on the second floor above Kinney's shoes, Orange Julius and a woman's fine apparel shop, Vic opened a sprawling 3,000-square-foot chrome-plated and red-carpeted gym for men and women.

Three walls were mirrored and one was windowed, overlooking the bustling Square below.

There's the Greyhound bus station (where's everybody goin'?) on the far side of the Lowe's Theater (*Psycho* is playing this week) and I can see three shiny banks on three different corners (money, who has money?). The world was growing fast.

I learned I disliked chrome weights; they're heavier and less friendly. Mirrors are obnoxious; they're depressing and distracting. Electronic devices with rolling wooden rollers or vibrating belts don't work; what were they thinking? Certain crowds are impossible: those liking chrome weights, mirrors and electronic devices.

I'd have quit, but they shut down only three months after I joined. Here today, gone tomorrow, like many health enthusiasts.

During my last year in Jersey, before heading for California, I would occasionally take a bus through the Lincoln Tunnel to the New York Port Authority and walk a block to Tommy Minichello's Mid-City Gym on 42nd Street.

Another upstairs gym, Mid-City expressed hard use, displayed no chrome, offered a few useless dusty and tarnished mirrors, and overlooked the colorful stream of hurrying New Yorkers seen, as I recall, through the heavy and rusting structure of a neon sign or a fire escape. My attention was on the weights.

I was in New York City, on the outer edge of my territory, among the tough guys. I kept busy, nodded and made friends with Tommy, mainly because he made friends with me. Heroes and the best of people are found in the strangest places. I always felt taller and stronger after training at Mid-City. I was among the tough guys—quiet, mild-mannered me. I survived, I grew.

You've heard enough about this next sanctuary in my bomber stories: The Dungeon, endless cracks in wide floors, high ceilings and tall walls; long narrow wooden staircases condemned by the unseen management yet frequently negotiated by brutes; rusting iron and splintered wood equipment in the dim light of night and day; passion and knowledge and understanding dripping down the walls and from the ceiling like the warm beer escaping the taps of the bar overhead; entry doors hanging askance by their remaining twisted hinges. The place was perfect in every way.

Over the years, I've collected an impressive file of tough workouts to review. You see, in 60 years, I rarely missed one…and none of them was easy. Training all out with meticulous form and mild sound effects always defined my style.

My most vivid tough workouts are set against the backdrop of the Muscle Beach Gym in the early 1960s. You have no idea how proud I am to have this theater and the real life plays that unfolded day after day as part of my experience. It's pure gold.

The magic didn't come from the pharmacist; it came from the soul, the era, the history in the making, the presence of un-compromised originality yet to be imitated.

My lifetime of workouts always bore a striking resemblance to that hardcore iron locomotion of years ago. It was in the Dungeon in 1963, '64, '65 and '66 that tough workouts took place. What kept me going without missing a beat is another story.

Later, I stayed for a month in Bondi Beach and walked five long blocks each morning to Paul Graham's gym in Sydney, Australia. I was there to promote bodybuilding and Paul was the promoter (among many other interesting and worthy things—some legendary— and too numerous to mention).

The gym reminded me of the Dungeon, except it was ground level. Big difference; I found the incoming light and nearness to civilization a distraction.

It was being in Australia clinging to the underside of Earth and working out with Paul and his buds that made the training each morning so memorable.

Apart from that, nothing changed—the same black, white and gray colors; the same used, time-darkened, generations-old steel; the same inventions and improvisations of crates, construction lumber and pipes; the same bench press, barbell curl, squat and deadlift, and the same recognizable groans of strange satisfaction. Our mates so far away didn't do it any differently than we did—guts and passion.

No wars with this mob.

When we weren't training at Paul's digs, we spent the mornings in Billy Moore's converted pigeon coop in Mascot, a quaint suburb of Sydney. How quaint can one get? The pigeons were relegated to the coops at the back of the property, while the sturdier sheds behind Billy's cottage were renovated to suit the humble needs of the local robust muscleheads. Another rugged patch of metal and hand-fabricated apparatus rose to the occasion: a gym built of necessity and desire.

You haven't trained until you've trained where pigeons once cooed, mated and pooped.

Now Serge Nubret's short subterranean gym was a place for only one workout. Again, under an old building on the corner of an old intersection in an old town, in this case Paris, where they speak French and do French things.

Drawbacks included a ceiling that was six feet high and lifting areas that were portioned into small rooms, each accessible by a 5′6″ doorway. Ducking was continual and I never stood erect—this is not easy on the back or good for the attitude. It was also dark and airless.

None of this troubled Serge. He was at once a prince and a pauper. He was also bench pressing 400 for reps on his second set while I was feeling my way along the walls and holding my forehead like a wounded soldier crawling off the battlefield in the night.

I worked out, but my movements were abbreviated and tense and felt eternal. I longed for the Dungeon, which had become an upscale penthouse in my mind.

Eventually, the featured gym of the Golden Era was Joe Gold's cinderblock bunker six feet off Pacific Avenue, a simple rectangle big enough for the sinewy handful interested in strain, pain and sacrifice in those early days.

It was clean, bright, airy, orderly, sufficiently spacious, reasonably jerk-free and emitted only gym noise. The dumbbells were plentiful, parked where they belonged, and the handles were thick. The bars were as straight as arrows and sat on racks of steel and rubber-matted platforms designated for heavy lifting. The plates were stored like precision machinery parts on stout plate racks. The equipment Joe built was made for rhinos: large pulleys, heavy cables, indestructible benches and big chinning and dipping bars.

Running toilets, showers and a drinking fountain topped off the amenities. A brute could be spoiled.

The place was built for building and build it did. Eventually a few gals showed up on the scene and we knew the times they were a changin.' Evolution and revolution took place within the four walls of Venice's Joe Gold's Gym, circa 1965 through the early '70s.

Now listen here, I saved the best for last: the World Gym in Santa Cruz, circa 1989. Every good thing one could put into a gym to build strong backs, strong minds and strong spirits we carefully installed in the World Gym of Santa Cruz and then duplicated two years later in Scotts Valley.

It was just the right size filled with Cybex, Hammer, Bodymaster, York and Ivanco, tall walls and high ceilings, a large loft to separately house the cardio equipment, simple colors in bold contrasts, order in layout and decoration in deference to busy-ness and trendy-ness in ornamentation, sound government to live by (no jerks, put your weights away, no cussing and no cell phones), cool music to boost not bust or burst the focused action on the floor and air from the ocean through the front door and out the back door.

I've run out of time, but not out of memorable gyms. Besides, I don't want to crowd your mind when you have gyms experiences of your own to recollect. Old memories can serve as fodder for inspiration, revived training plans, lost hope and renewed enthusiasm.

You can leave the hangar doors unlocked when you go; no one will steal anything. It's all free anyway.

WHEN THE STICK BROKE

I'm just a guy from Jersey who likes to work out and happened to win Mr. America doin' weight lifting. I started with pushups, chins and dips like scrawny kids do, bummed some weights when I was 12 and messed around with 'em until I was outta high school. Then I joined a YMCA, learned a few tricks, moved to California and learned a few more. I trained regularly, I grew, I ate, trained hard, grew some more, trained harder, ate more protein and sorta got cut.

Bingo, won a few contests.

People want to know how I did it, what'd I do, what'd I eat, what's the secret. Fact is, I just answered all the questions in the above paragraph. I think it's computers and technology that has us complicating things, asking a million questions and needing a million answers. When does anybody have time to work out after looking for all the answers and heaping up all the information?

I admire that information gathering, that quest, that inquisitiveness, that internal and external need to know: fascinating, challenging, fulfilling and enriching, absorbing and endless. Me? One more set and you can have the bench, thanks.

Over the years I've rambled on about the training routine I'd do if I had to do it all over again, perhaps shedding a little light on our favorite subject. And sometimes (often), I fell short. I must try harder to make myself understood.

We don't lift weights to achieve mass, power and speed one month and start scrimmage the next—tackles, passes, touchdowns and cheerleaders. After a winter with the iron, it's not batting practice in the spring with mitts and bats and balls and beers. The benefits of improved strength and endurance gained from tough hours in the weight room are not enjoyed while we test our talents and develop our skills on the rings, high bar or track and field.

We don't lift weights for a season. We lift weights now, later, again and again, once more, another time, today, tomorrow, the next day, and repeat next week.

Between workouts, we think of working out and rest, repair, wait, plan and hope and scrutinize much too much. Then it's back to the iron and steel, sets and reps, monotony and speculation, perseverance, discipline, patience and doubt.

Why did I superset? Why did I perform volume training? Because I liked it that way. I liked the pace, the rhythm, the flow, the perfection of form, the athletic feel, the etching repetition, the dance, the busyness, the involvement, the pump, the burn, the efficiency, the cardiorespiratory application, the high.

I noticed I was always able to add hard muscle by eating big and smartly. I was always able to employ a more complete percentage of my muscle tissue with a locomotion of sets and reps performed with exact full range of motion, intensity and zeal. My first rep was thoughtful and deliberate; my last rep thoughtful, deliberate and red-zone intense. The volume delivers maximum-force saturation, maximum muscle involvement.

I'm a slave.

Why did I always mix in heavy days with deads, squats, power curls and presses throughout the month? I like the strain, the mighty exertion, the challenge, the force of will, the aloneness of concentration, the pause and focus and grapple of determination, the gravity and poised iron, the total body-mind execution, the play, the white-light approach to the single and the trembling darkness after the single is completed. I recommend the power moves because I like the power, the mass and the thickness they encourage.

Why did I mix everything in my loose fashion? First, why miss any of it if you can have it all? Second, because I like to and because it works for me. I think we stumbled onto something here—perhaps something we can all agree on, the most enlightening truth learned throughout the years of wildly spinning these word strings.

We're all different and we all need different methods of training. What works for you may not work for me, and vice-versa. Too simplistic? No, no it's not. Actually, it's perfect in its simplicity.

Some folks know the chemistry, the physics, the physiology, the hormones, the fast twitch and slow twitch, the research, the theory and the science. Still, the questions are posed and the answers are parroted.

Over the years, I've noted that there's nothing new that has surfaced in science or experience or experiment that can alter my original training philosophy and habits for the better.

I'm open enough. There's just nothing there. Lots of ideas, styles, hype arguments and misunderstanding.

Give me the iron and let me soak. Most of what I read today provides reinforcement of the basic and simple practices I've applied from the 1960s forward.

A lot of folks grow angry and disappointed when the progress is slow. Look, it's always slow. It's always going to be slow, so relax.

MUSCLEHEADS I HAVE KNOWN

What is it that attracts us to lifting weights? Upon first consideration the deep thinker tosses out a few standard responses and expects to move on to more scintillating things of the mind. To build muscle and strength and improve one's health is the classic answer to the inquiry, yet is not nearly sufficient.

The one-liner summarizes what weightlifting does, but only scratches the surface of why one lifts the iron. A long and comprehensive list of reasons unfolds as the question is more thoroughly addressed and the question that appeared simple becomes complex.

We're all different, agreed, but I'm certain there are basic reasons mixed with obvious attractions and blended with simple purposes… and, um…needs and desires, cures and fixes, neuroses and illusions, pleasures and pains and goals all lifters—muscleheads—share in common. Sounds like lifting weights makes nuclear science look like coloring by numbers.

A musclehead is anyone who lifts weights regularly, has done so for years and feels crazy when he doesn't. "Musclehead" is a complimentary term—a crown ascribed only to the worthy, a fact not everyone is aware of, including often the musclehead himself.

All shapes, all sizes, all goals, what a group!

Some seek to mold a beautiful body, others are content to chisel away the daily stress and strife of life. One mounts the pounds and packs on the mass, another settles for focus, form and deep concentration. She seeks to lose fat and gain muscle, he seeks to gain weight and lose fat, and they both seek confidence and self-esteem.

You can get huge and ripped, fast and strong, and healthy and fit, but as for me, let me dwell amid the metal, feel the steel, feed the deed and wait upon the weights.

Beyond muscleheads and musclehead madness, there are ironheads and ironhead insanity. Observe.

During my years of training hither and yon, I occasionally looked up from my task and noticed the characters across the gym floor. Fascinating! They, unlike this ordinary and conventional writer, are the weirdest of creatures doing the strangest of things. Let me give you a rundown of some characters I've known; perhaps you've come across them in your own treks along the narrow pathways and broad highways of lifting weights and pushing iron.

~ She's 30ish, solid and marches into the gym as if on a mission of life and death. She orders an espresso as she signs in, and is off to the locker room like a quick-change artist. In gear—leather belt around the waist, gloves on the hands, headband and assorted wraps in place—this determined and unstoppable feminine force downs the thick, hot black drink in a gulp as she eyes the gym floor, her target.

Equipment is set up with alacrity to serve her multiple-set training routine: a bench with pairs of 30s, 25s, 20s and 15s arranged geometrically before it, and the bench press with an Olympic bar and 10-pound plates. She lays a small towel on the bench to discourage other gym members from using it, and her drinking bottle sits on the bench before the four pair of idle dumbbells. Having marked her territory, she's breathing heavy, needs a rest and someone to talk to. There's John.

They talk. She talks, he listens. She talks, he sits and listens. She talks, he ceases to listen and glances about looking for help. People are stepping over her weights and walking around her benches and no one is getting anything done—not her, her nervous prey, nor the inconvenienced, now seething mob of co-trainees.

I've seen this person return the dumbbells without ever using them, and leave the gym without ever training. In a year, she gained 20 pounds she didn't want, couldn't explain, doesn't need and will never use. She passed like a ship in the night. What was that all about?

~ It's early and the town sleeps. The door to the Dungeon is closed as tightly as possible, a gap of less than an inch remaining between the two twisted, overlapping doors. He's here. No one forces the huge and ancient doors into such a final position except him.

I assert myself and pull the doors open with great effort and practiced finesse. I stand at the entrance peering downward and listen to the hollow silence, warm air from the depths escaping into the dark morning. A clang, another and then the great rumble begins. It's all so ridiculous.

I descend the staircase and the source of the calamity stands before me under the shadowy light of a 40-watt bulb hanging by a chord from the blackness of the high ceiling. The man is fierce, 330 pounds of meat on a 5′10″ frame, and covered in a collection of torn and ragged sweat clothes, remnants from years of merciless tearing and tugging and gnawing.

One hand at shoulder level grasps a thick bar attached to a column for support; the other hand holds a colossal dumbbell low to the ground between bent legs. The stance indicates the completion of an exercise in strength, but is in reality the starting position for repetition, one-arm power cleans, the large man's version of the single, side-arm lateral raise.

He commences another of six reps with a shrill and mighty roar—a piteous, howling scream of torment, really—and the action is... terrifying. Pounding flesh shows through the wrappings and the traps are unmistakable, starting behind the ears and bulging as they reach for the deltoid's outer limits.

"Hey, brother," we exchange greetings, polite maniacs, and blend into the welcome darkness of the Dungeon. It'll be daylight soon and the hideous sounds will once again come to an end. We're both mild-mannered guys in real life.

I ask you again, "What attracts a person to lifting weights?"

Ask him? I dare you.

~ Then there was my first real live California training partner. I wasn't in town a week before I hooked up with the man, eight years my senior, and began blasting it with new ammunition and artillery. Dick Sweet was a recent Mr. California title-holder and as slick and lean as one could only get naturally: no look-alike physique, no puff, no over-sized muscle parts, no chemicals, no short cuts—very cool and very sweet. At a ripped 190 pounds, he matched my strength at a balloony 240.

What I knew about training could fill a thimble and what he knew and understood could scarcely be contained in a reservoir. And so my learning commenced.

This guy was meticulous, not in dress, though he looked ruggedly neat in his t-shirt covered with an extra-large hooded sweatshirt, over which he wore a double-extra-large long-sleeve flannel shirt. Precision, rather, defined his every movement: perfection in form, careful order in sets and repetitions and exactness of pace and timing.

At first glance, rigidness in training appears stiff, intellectual, unfriendly and excessively demanding. Upon continued performance, the most accurate word to describe the training style is "disciplined."

Discipline is a master; stiff, intellectual and excessive are foolishness. One must become disciplined to understand it. Practice, application, observation, patience, hard work and assiduousness are pathways to discipline. Achieve discipline and the tall mountain becomes a lush plane. I discovered these things at the side of my dauntless and unswerving partner over the course of two years within the meditative confines of the Muscle Beach Dungeon.

Benches were raised by one-inch, two-inch and three-inch blocks to achieve the exact angle to affect muscle recruitment. Felt good. Plaster was surgically removed from center-floor columns to accommodate one's backside, thus preventing excess thrust and producing a precise arch to the back for perfect execution when performing upright side-arm lateral raises. Worked great. The angled preacher-curl bench was tipped forward and stabilized to attain a more demanding, less threatening peak biceps movement. What an advantage.

Intelligent improvising of equipment, creative modifying of movements and selective supersetting of exercises expanded training into a friendly, personalized process. Everything was made to fit.

Time between sets was not idle; it was strategically arranged, utilized and focused. We breathed to recuperate and positioned equipment for upcoming exercises while psychologically preparing for the subsequent sets. The body's responses were assessed and recorded for further referral.

And the joy of training was not lost for a minute. We knew why we trained, how we trained and sought ways to improve our training, which was in no way shabby. We knew it and acknowledged it with appropriate humility. We were respectfully aware of the guys in the shadows of other gyms who were bigger, stronger and, er...badder.

Intensity within each set and rep was searched out and realized. Nothing we determined to do was left undone. I followed the serious man about the dark, gloomy and damp space below ground level like it was a brilliant mountain top. My eagerness and Jersey innocence fed his hip California, destination-bound nature.

Together, we unburied treasures with our bare hands and stored them in our souls.

The 20-stair descent to the floor of the Dungeon held apprehension every morning those years. I trained six days a week, mostly with that original training partner, and never missed a beat. Each workout was to exceed the last. The pressure was self-imposed and mounted day after day. The titles came and went.

The reps, the sets came and went. The days and nights came and went. My time with Dick…went. I often wonder where that dude is today.

Between the two of us, we can list a hundred reasons why we train.

~ There are the loud mouths in every gym who bang the weights around, drop the dumbbells and leave plates lying around the floor. They deserve to be punished and I suspect they are eventually. Who cares why they lift weights?

~ How about the guy sitting on the leg press wearing earphones and reading on his phone? I have mixed emotions: gratitude, thankful I'm not him, shallow and unmotivated; and contempt, wanting to express my loathing with a mild shot of a taser to the butt. Why am I so intolerant? Vapid personalities sap energy and permeate the gym atmosphere with indolence and indifference. That's why! Zap zap zap!

Don't ask why he lifts, he hasn't noticed.

~ Some of my best friends are personal trainers, but some of their clients try my soul. The guy sits on the bench as the trainer hands him the dumbbells, one by one. He performs the set as instructed and the trainer removes the iron devices from shaky, dutiful hands. The trainee follows the trainer to the bench press where he sits as the trainer slides on the appropriate plates. The trainee watches passively and fiddles with his shoelace.

The set is performed—you can do this, big set, push it, one more rep—and the weight is replaced like a large book upon a bookshelf.

The handle for the pulley machine is chosen by the trainer and attached to the cable's end. The weight stack is assessed and adjusted by the trainer. The exercise is executed with clinical precision by the other guy, and they move on to the Swiss ball for crunches and stretches and rolly-polly wobblies.

They don't get it and they never will, not as long as they sit in the back seat and leave the driving to the tour guide.

There's joy in independence, and the freedom and growth that accompanies the rich quality. To choose your own dumbbells, to firmly grasp and retrieve them from the rack and haul them to the bench is one's duty—and the precursor to a fulfilling set of intense reps. Do it.

They're getting it. They're doing it.

Mankind does not live by sets and reps alone. We live and become more by separating, distinguishing, combining and installing many elements and components together to form the whole.

The challenge is in all of it, not some of it: the calculating, the choosing, the deciding, the carrying to and fro, the loading and unloading, the counting, the struggling, the winning and losing.

Learn the ABCs from an expert; discover the XYZs on your own and become the expert.

Which brings us to the end of the alphabet, bombers.

THE TRAINING STYLES OF OUR HEROES

Here you are reading my point of view, some clean advice, but by no means the last or only word. I'm a bodybuilder. I encourage full ranges of motion with full extension and full contraction for the majority of the repetitions. I prefer moderate to heavy poundage with higher reps—eight to twelve—to maximize the involvement of the entire body and all the fiber types.

With moderate weight and a mix of reps, I'm able to set a groove and incorporate a solid body-thrust technique that brings more muscle groups into play and creates a rhythm in the repetitions. Though I practiced single-set training on occasion, have a lifetime of accenting my workouts with supersets and trisets.

We all have our own training styles, and yours is developing as you read this and other training material, observe others in action and experiment on your own. In that smelly weight room, you crawl under a bar loaded with seemingly immovable iron plates that clank and proceed to lift them up and down for 6, 8, 10…15 repetitions, more if your joints, muscles and oxygen hold out.

Then, with no one looking or caring, you replace the massive mess with a crash, sit up and, like a fool, add more weight to the sagging the bar. Time to kill, you sit on the edge of the bench and focus on the next thrilling expenditure of energy and strength, knowing pain is necessary to achieve advancement in the sport of your dreams.

Five sets of this muscle-building exercise and you can move on to another and another and another. There's the one where you bend over and lift, and the one where you stand and push, not to mention the one where you sit and pull. How about the one where you load the big dumb bar on your back and go up and down with your wobbly legs 'till you want to die? That's always good for a few cheers from the bleachers.

Let's add a few more plates—nickels, dimes, quarters and halves—like they were money and we were rich. Spot me, man, I'm going for a single.

We all do that sometimes. Now what about the differences?

I trained around Arnold for a few years when we shared similar training methods, which enhanced us both. Yet, in our arm training, we went our separate ways. Arnold gains massive and proportionate biceps and triceps through muscle isolation, pumping and burning. I prefer heavier weight with a full range of motion to involve the body more entirely.

Frank Zane and I met at the gym every morning at sunrise to train midsection and either chest, back or shoulders. Yet our arm and leg workouts didn't match—I have more difficulty and require more work in these areas than Frank.

Franco Columbu and I co-trained successfully, though his strength in pressing far exceeded mine and we differed in pace. Tom Platz trained hard, often to the extreme. In his radical performance, he often went to complete failure, sometimes doing a bodypart workout consisting of a single set of 50 or perhaps a hundred excruciating reps.

Dave Johns and I trained in Europe for several weeks and I experienced his awesome power in the bench and squat. As he worked, slow and heavy, I often did three sets while he prepared to do one massive set, moving a mountain to my foothills.

When I met Sergio Oliva in New York City, he was practicing Olympic lifting to thicken and shape his entire body. Ken Waller did reps with 400 on the bench and 500 in the squat, yet for shoulders and arms, I've known him to use lightweight, angular movements and isolation. The very patient Lee Labrada has similar, highly specialized, concentrated techniques to gain fine muscle detail.

I've known Leroy Colbert to do literally a hundred sets of upper-body exercises, and watched Zabo and friends spend both morning and afternoon doing as many sets of full squats. At the other end of the spectrum, we saw Mike Mentzer grow and grow on his intense, single-set Heavy Duty System.

I could go on and on with great fun describing the variety of training styles I've shared with my partners and peers over the years and in vastly different training venues. From a converted pigeon coop in Sydney, to Serge Nubret's subterranean cubicles in Paris, I've sorted my way through a maze of crazy workouts. They all seem to work if one's heart is in there, so suit yourself after some trial and testing.

Much of what I've learned has come from observing people in action on the gym floor, an extraordinary cross-section of people training with purpose and good intentions. As I looked out over a gym's square footage, observed the variety of activity and listened to the range of questions thrown my way, I'm convinced that flow and continuity in training should be encouraged from the beginning.

Once a new lifter completes the first weeks of introductory exercise and gets a feel for the equipment, muscle resistance and personal level of condition, let's practice interesting exercise combinations to piece the workouts together.

I'd get them supersetting right away, where two or more exercises that complement each other are performed one after another to enhance lifting output. This multi-set training not only condenses workout time; it also increases productivity considerably.

Single-set training has its place in workouts and should be retained for strength building. And a training scheme blended with superset combinations adds excitement and dimension to a daily routine.

Supersetting is a technique I applied for more than 60 years (gulp) and one I put into use long before reading a muscle magazine or going to a gym. I instinctively gravitated toward a nonstop training style to maintain enthusiasm and momentum.

Without the downtime between sets, we become more involved in our training. There's no time for daydreaming—wishing to be somewhere else—or for boredom. In fact, a most desirable attitude of training develops, one that we wrongly texpect to be reserved for athletes on the fringe of competition. This attitude of training is a valuable tool of confidence and will provide a very real psychological benefit for you.

With a little time and a little practice your training becomes more athletic as you move through the gym from one exercise to another. Your heart rate remains higher, you stay warmer as you near the edge of aerobic training, concentration becomes locked and the harmony of movements lures you onward.

Why do I mix styles in my loose fashion? First, why miss any of it if you can have it all? It's like building a house of stones of differing size to accommodate shear pressure, material availability, rugged appearance and the joy of building.

Second, I like it and it works for me. We're all different and we all need different methods of training. What works for me may not work for you.

It's not, "You go your way and I'll go mine. See ya." It's not "My way or the highway; your way or no way." We're on the foothills together. Any one of us can get to the mountaintop by desire, faith, trial, logic, failure and persistence. We can all get there by encouragement from one another, spirit and humility.

Someone asked me if I supersetted regularly in my early years of training. As I recall, I applied the classic East Coast approach to building muscle, a style one may very well call "onslaught training."

You position yourself roughly before a barbell and with little warning, you pounce on it and beat it to the ground. Breathing heavily, crouching and circling, you grab the dumbbells in a power lock, twist, pummel and, as before, slam them down without mercy.

Always on the move, sweating and cursing, you hold your rusty pig iron opponent at arm's length before performing an excruciating overhead press, a crushing barbell drop set and, finally, the backbreaking deadlift. No whimpering, no reason, no questions, no excuses, no witnesses.

All that stuff came years later.

I moved to California and refined my moves, put order in my workouts and began to use primarily superset techniques. I got a handle on protein, fats and carbs and bore the yoke like an ox on the threshing floor, season after season.

For three years the bulk of my training was hard and heavy and my bodyweight hovered like a blimp at 245 pounds, a significant mound at the time. My workouts went three hours from 6:00 to 9:00 in the morning, six days a week times 52 weeks a year.

I used a popular 12, 10, 8, 6, 4 rep scheme most frequently on major moves, with the 6 to 8 rep standard managing secondary movements and change-of-pace days. I always worked forearms and did maximum weight repetitions of various moves every third week to apply the muscle to the max.

Through the years, I tried every technique and muscle-group combination, various splits, high reps and low, and regularly came back to beefy workouts with last-rep intensity, providing form is B+ and joints and muscle connections weren't severely compromised. On occasion, of course, one must pay the executioner.

I was constantly moving, set-to-set, actively recuperating and psyching or arranging equipment for the next combination. Though

I'm driven, I don't rush. I like time to immerse myself in my workout—I average 70 miles per hour in the 65 lane. When I'm done, I'm done.

If we listed the essential information we gained over the years, would it stack to the top of a very tall squat rack? Or would it settle into a pile no higher than an average household's incoming mail, junk excluded. How much have we really learned? What do we know?

What did John Grimek know about building muscle that he didn't invent? What did Steve Reeves know that he didn't acquire from the grains of sand of Muscle Beach? Reg Park—who taught him in the shadows of his old English garage?

Bill Pearl learned all he needed to know about weightlifting in the hull of a Navy ship and the streets of Oakland. Arnold and Franco pushed heavy weights, ate steak and eggs, and laughed and played without requests, as sure as the California sun.

That cast of characters plays the starring roles in the original drama of bodybuilding. Today, via the trusty, real-life muscle mags and their social media streams, eager physical culturists watch the barbell soaps, hard-body sitcoms, muscular sci-fis and mostly the "get huge fast" commercials. Confounding questions are posed, each with a dozen equivocal answers. We ponder as we enter the gym, confused, spent and beleaguered. Who am I and what am I doing here?

Ignore for a minute, able as you are, the enormous pressure of information and data. Chances are good, should you be locked long enough in a garage full of weights, you'd come out huge and ripped. Or if you're stranded on an uninhabited island, you'll look for a place to do chins, dips and rock lifts. You'll build the best body in the land.

The only thing to stop this from happening would be finding a tattered book that told you how to do it in 30 days.

BULKING UP IS HARD TO DO

When I won Mr. New Jersey in the spring of 1963, I stood onstage among a throng of big, fat guys by today's standards. We were all training hard and heavy and eating like apes. There were lats and chests, shoulders and biceps everywhere; thighs were a bit light and there were no calves anywhere unless one was born with them. The few guys who had abs stood out, not for their unusual muscularity, but because they were skinny—fleas with muscles.

It was Jersey, after all, and these were the beginnings.

Looking back at my childhood, teens and the few years of adulthood before moving to California, I see a guy growing up on meat and potatoes. Not bad. The gooey stuff, cupcakes, Three Musketeers, jelly beans, soda pop, Fudgsicles and chocolate chip cookies, oozed through my body during the reckless summers at the lake before my teen years, and sugar accompanied by the rancid fat of the all-beef hotdogs was pure fuel. Swim, run, jump, row, paddle, hike and race.

I recycled the junk into action and carbon dioxide.

Most of the time, my two older brothers and I ate our meat and potatoes and a vegetable at dinner as a family, and my mom made sure we each took our vitamins and minerals—the spindly framework of order and discipline was pieced together. I wasn't up against the world's worst habits from the starting blocks, thank God. Early influences and habits define, and given half a chance, they can make or break.

I was consciously force-feeding at 20, when bulking up had become my burden of choice, my expression, my plan of attack; the un-crowded road I'd travel for a long time to come. I found myself living on the outskirts of society with a bunch of guys and their wives, girls and families. A collection of real decent folk with common interests; they liked to lift weights, be strong and build their muscles.

They also ate well and preferred to go about their own business without the interruption of conventional distractions and responsibilities.

Pure and simple, they were a subculture of muscleheads: postal workers, university students, school teachers, a doctor, a lawyer or two, an engineer, a pilot, a few wrestlers, more than one actor and a lot of extras. We mingled, like-minded and private, encouraging and respectful: have muscles, will travel.

Some of us bulked up together. Across the street from the Muscle Beach Gym on 4th and Broadway in Santa Monica hid The Little Inn, an all-you-can-eat Swedish smorgasbord no bigger than a newsstand.

After our evening workout, a handful of us would plod over to the Inn and make our way around the center-island steamer table and salad bar. The management looked at us with despair as we made our way around the all-you-can-eat serving table with our sleeves rolled up and "hunger" tattooed on our foreheads. We grazed and talked and planned and eventually fell silent…stuffed.

Our plates were always empty when we left, tables cleared with final gulps of water before we funneled out the door, leaving behind us a collective sigh of relief from the owner-chef manager and needlessly intimidated diners.

At nearly 250 pounds, I was at a svelte weight compared to the company of huge men with whom I associated. Chuck Fish, aspiring strong man and pro wrestler weighed 330; Chuck Ahrens was 330 under several sweatshirts and the widest man I've ever seen in my life; legendary Steve Merjanian weighing 320 and carrying the weight with inspiring symmetry (he could move more iron in an hour than a locomotive); and Oliver Sacks from England who trained at the Dungeon while attending graduate school at UCLA.

Oliver weighed over 300 pounds, was brilliant, and told fascinating stories with a remarkable talent for describing people, places and things. He's the same Oliver Sacks who was an acclaimed neurologist and author of award-winning fiction and non-fiction, including *Awakenings*. The face on the book jacket looks like him, only he's thinner and older and no longer wearing a shredded spinnaker for a shirt.

Not yet 30, Oliver was a massive man who looked as scholarly as any rogue wandering the back allies of town in his torn-out sweatshirt, bearded face and unkempt hair. His motorcycle reminded me of a junkyard dog, gnarly, beat up and vicious. I respected Oliver because he moved the iron like a crane. He squatted, deadlifted and bench pressed with the best of the coast's powerlifters, not to set records, but to set his sights; not to raise his image, but to raise his spirits; not to prove something, but to resist gravity with all his might for the joy of it.

His interest was not in what he did, but in what he was doing.

My respect for Dr. Sacks turned to admiration while sitting at a tiny table in a dimly lit corner of the restaurant, where we were eating Swedish meatballs. He told of his recent excursions around the powerlifting circuit, stories of huge men "with deltoids the size and consistency of cantaloupes performing lifts so extraordinary that tempered steel bars twisted under the weight, the great breaths of air exhaled by the mighty men causing small dust clouds on the edges of the lifting platform."

I was 22 years old and never before had I heard life presented so vividly in lilting prose and accented in educated British. What manner of man dwells beneath a ragged sweatshirt the size of a tent?

How many miles, how many galaxies Ollie has traveled since that most unforgettable moment a lifetime ago?

In the continuing quest for muscle, Thursday night was a grand meat and seafood all-you-can-eat buffet at Ted's Rancho, a long and narrow restaurant overhanging a beach in Malibu, and Sunday was a brunch at The Sea Lion, an eatery a mile farther north on the same Coast Highway. These were bargain feasts for bulkers, and I have fond memories of my frequent visits as I tramped along to my goal of 250 pounds.

For me, the process of gaining mass covered a five-year span to age 22, improving in efficiency as I practiced, learned and increased in strength—proceeding to lift heavier and harder. At no time did I let up. I ate a lot, but I didn't pig out on sugar or carbs. Whatever protein I could reach and fat I couldn't trim was cast into the furnace for workouts and muscle growth.

To the young guys over the years who wanted to gain weight, I'd often give the eat-a-lot-of-wholesome-food-frequently program. Three weeks later, distraught and downtrodden, they'd confess that they "can't seem to put on a pound." I guess they didn't have enough time and were attempting to accelerate the cumbersome weight-gain procedure by heavy fretting and by applying substantial disappointment.

I failed to include in the program a primary imperative: for a long time. How long? As long as it takes.

It's two more sets of heavy fretting and substantial disappointment before the truth sinks in: They're on their own.

I hope they don't walk away from the gym and find themselves eventually trying to dig their way out of obesity like an awful lot of their parents and friends who never stood in a gym, but do regularly eat a lot, frequently...and for a long time. They're on their own, also.

Bulking up is hard to do. Becoming overweight is easy. Caution: Don't confuse the two.

MY BUMPER, KNUCKLE HEAD

A bell from somewhere sounded 12 times. Midnight in Manhattan is neither late nor early; it's just another hour of the day.

Nickel's Steak House is down a dark side street off Broadway. All streets off Broadway are dark compared to the brilliant and stunning excitement of the grandest intersection in the world. The steaks were exceptional, the day long and hard, the contest crowd a crazy blur and the announcement of our victories a bonanza one cannot presume. Our appearances at The Old Townhouse where Dan Lurie held his annual bodybuilding spectaculars in the 1970s were complete and we were, for the moment, content.

Leaving the Steak House, our trophies and gym bags in tow, four of us—Boyer Coe, Ralph Kroger, Tony Schettino and me— casually, almost aimlessly, headed to our hotel rooms. We crossed the narrow street diagonally under a street lamp that dumped its light on the dimmed storefronts and tightly parked cars below.

What's with the guy in the tux standing in the shadows with the two women dressed to kill? No doubt the threesome wondered what was with the four guys the size of trucks coming their way. No matter. They stood their ground, looking dismayed and fretful. The end of their evening—or was it the beginning?—had taken a turn for the worse. The car belonging to them was a white snappy thing perfectly wedged between a Buick and a Chrysler.

We stared as Tuxman got behind the wheel and gunned the engine as if it were a tractor about to roll over the mere obstacles and be on his merry way, pretty ladies and all.

"Excuse me, sir," I said as I bent over and peaked in his window, "We'll help you."

He snarled and gave it his best shot until lady-in-red pleaded for her bumper, "My bumper!"

Tuxman, as red as the lady-in-red's dress, crawled out of the car and turned to us. The remnants of enthusiasm for a cause calling for muscle and might gathered beneath our ruddy brows, plus a reserve of adrenalin to meet the task.

Powerlifters all, at one time or another, we assembled at the appropriate corners of the immovable vehicle. It's all the same, iron and steel—a grip where necessary, the back and legs and arms in synchronized tightness: the count, ready, one, two, lift, move…and down. Again, ready, one, two, lift, move and down.

In five consecutive shifts, we had the little white darling in the middle of the street and pointing in the right direction. We didn't say much; what's to say? They bounded out of there like gazelle freed from a cage in a jungle.

We picked up our gear and resumed our jaunt in the general direction of home. Tony unwrapped his doggy bag and began to chew on the meaty bone of his leftovers.

"What time's your flight, Draper?"

AS OLD AS THE HILLS

Musclebuilding is as old as the hills. When man first realized women were attracted to slick, muscular bodies, and discovered rocks, prey, mischievous cave-dwellers and monsters were lifted more easily with a mighty back and strong arms, man put his genius to work, and thus his body, to improve his sinewy assets. The Dinosaur Championships held in 10,000 BC crowned the original Mr. World, and records were established in rock snatches and boulder clean-and-jerks.

The movement had begun and the next thing we knew, John Grimek was Mr. America and Steve Reeves was making *Hercules* films. This muscle stuff is becoming popular; there's a subculture budding in the grungy YMCAs and garages around the world—bodybuilding's spreading to the sunny beaches of California and before long will be mainstream.

During the 1950s Muscle Beach in Santa Monica emerged as the muscle and physical culture capital of the world.

And so the stage is set for the West Coast bodybuilding scene, that time in the history of weightlifting when bodybuilding neared critical mass, swirled in its growing energy and attracted its grand external source of power, the spectators. It was the Golden Era of bodybuilding, new, young, alive, untainted, unworn, unexploited...and adored. The spectators became fans.

This was a particular group of people with a special interest who inhabited a small region of California during a short period of time. Dick Tyler experienced, observed and recorded this golden stretch of bodybuilding history between 1965 and 1971 as a journalist, as a participant and as a weight lifting devotee. His eyes and ears were acute and his love for the sport was wrapped up in an affectionate sense of humor, the most accurate and appealing conduit of delivery for this unique physical expression.

You see, bodybuilding is a sport, an art form, a diversion, a hobby, an obsession, a competition, a love affair and a lifestyle.

Things heated up around the world in the '60s. Life became restless. Emotions and passions of the sensitive and few picked up the undercurrent, responded to the vibe. Men looked for something to hold onto, to keep them ready and balanced, directed and challenged yet entertained. Iron and steel, muscle and might emerged.

Alas, Muscle Beach, too wonderful to endure, sadly unraveled. Individuals surfaced in its place and what simmered for years was ready to erupt in slow motion.

We watched the passionate explosion of events from the lens of the cameras whose shutters were triggered at the most perfect moments by artists Russ Warner and Artie Zeller. Few photographers have witnessed in their viewfinders the vivid story that was about to unfold. Those same picture-takers engendered the events, stimulated bodybuilding's progress, universally popularized physical fitness and recorded the sport's stunning occasions now known as history.

There were only a handful of weightlifters, powerlifters and bodybuilders during this natural period of bodybuilding development. And in the US, three men and their magazines—Peary Rader with *Ironman,* Bob Hoffman with *Strength and Health* and Joe Weider with *Muscle Builder*—sought to expand the sport and popularize its participants.

Popularize soon became known as capitalize. It was during the Golden Era when the machinery of competition and marketing magnified and amplified the activities of muscle and might, iron and steel, and went on to create the rather large pool of spectators and participants of all shapes and sizes we know today.

Bodybuilding, once a puppy with a waggily tail, had become a monster. I do not say this without affection. Monsters can be cute.

I had the precious advantage (graced by God, actually) of being in the middle of it all. And I'm still in the middle of it all. The years have come and gone and tons of weights have moved up and down. I, as you, love this stuff and I can't, nor do I wish to, put it aside.

This was not a history from which we learn, but memories in which to share and delight. There was a marriage in the minds and souls of Dick and Artie and Russ and others that cannot be duplicated. Their synergy provided an insight into a beautiful past that no historian or scholar could ever understand.

ARTIE ZELLER, AN ORIGINAL

I met Artie during my first week in Santa Monica, California. In helping George Eiferman run things for Joe Weider in his new baby West Coast operation, I would roll bins full of processed mail order items out the back door to the postal loading ramps, where they'd be weighed, stamped and marked for delivery.

Artie was the postman and it was there we started our long friendship. My life was to be enriched by Artie, his camera, his unmatched wit, his meticulousness, his bright insight, his generosity, his loyalty.

Zeller was a manifest original. He grew up in New York City, not far from Coney Island, where he blasted the weights and built a symmetrical and handsome physique when there were very few around.

He was an anomaly who lived 30 years in the postal agency, patiently, serenely as if the days and hours were a pause, a means to get on with the real part of his life with enthusiasm and expression.

His candid black and white photography of the late 1960s and early '70s documented bodybuilding's irretrievable Golden Years, a history we enjoy like warm apple pie.

Zeller, along with another hero, Russ Warner, cradled bodybuilding in their Roloflexes and presented it to the world for all to see and thus to know. And by the master photographers' hands, we watched bodybuilding's personality grow.

Artie had two loves greater than his camera and his Muscle Beach haunts. His wife Josie starred in his life…and he played brilliant chess, often trading moves with famous board prodigy, Bobby Fisher.

If you're a true bodybuilder, remember this: The next time you see a Zeller photo, you're looking at a masterpiece.

Not long after Artie died, I sat before the computer and answered every last email: how to gain muscle, how to lose fat. Andro this. Sterol that. Been bodybuilding for two weeks and nothing's happening, no cuts, no mass.

Eventually, the email counter read -0- …zero. I quickly shut down, stepped back and momentarily stared at the screen. Cherish the moment.

I love the email I get. It's the voice of an audience. But when it mounts while I sleep, it makes me dizzy. The fact is, the email I get is exceptional—real people, real lives, real loves, frustrations, problems, delights and discoveries. Thank you, it's a privilege.

I eventually dashed off enough cyber answers to clean the cyber slate, headed for LA and an occasion we'll never forget. Gathered in a bright and airy room overlooking a central square in Venice was a collection of the Muscle Beach and Golden Age originals.

Lou Ferrigno and Arnold were two of the youngest of about a hundred who came together to honor the Artie's memory, remembering a beautiful guy who told the story of bodybuilding to everyone, everywhere through his photography. You know his work; it's your favorite black and white candid pictures that depict the age of bodybuilding before it rolled over.

Everyone knew each other; everyone genuinely embraced—everyone a character with history and miles. There was great food and refreshments and excited conversations. Point and shoot cameras were constantly being produced and engaged.

Eventually John Balik of *IronMan* spoke and set in motion a series of spontaneous eulogies from an emotional congregation. Arnold told of Artie's mentoring, and had us rolling on the floor with his

Zeller imitations and stories. They spent a lot of time together and were tight.

Joe Weider was beside himself, and Gregory Hines couldn't hold back the tears. Mostly, we laughed, and nodded, and agreed we were a family that had captured a priceless moment in time.

Artie Zeller was, indeed, a most unforgettable character, an original, un-duplicatable. His life was defined by his love for Josie, his camera, and his far-reaching friendships of the bodybuilding world—a curious world that spanned half a century.

Artie's first years as a bodybuilder were spent pumping iron with Marvin Eder on Coney Island in the crazy New York City territory. He particularly loved Santa Monica and Venice Beach, his haunts during most of these fascinating years.

Artie's wonder and keen insight bore holes in the social landscape in which he dwelled. He didn't miss a tone or shade of the life that surrounded him.

Look at his black and white photography and understand. You don't see a paper photo; you see a story and feel a mood and hear voices and are compelled to listen. They're a moment, still yet continuing. His honest composition takes you there and you don't care to leave.

What is a man without his sense of humor? Artie considered every issue carefully and had strong and bright convictions. At the same time he found comedy in almost everything, never silly, sometimes cynical, but mostly laughably funny.

His favorite stories center on his photo shoots, Joe Weider, and the beloved bodybuilders. There's the one where a splotch of us were positioned before Artie's precise lens on Venice Beach—muscular, tan and perfectly lit by the fading day's-end sun.

Joe Weider was directing activities with great passion, "Artie, Artie, shoot the picture."

“Joe, I’m out of film,” replied Zeller.

“Artie, I don’t care! Shoot it anyway!” Joe yelped, jumping and flailing his arms.

Artie’s camera clicked and all was quiet.

RUSS WARNER—A MOST UNFORGETTABLE CHARACTER

I don't know enough about Russ Warner to write his biography, but I can tell you he lived a full life until the day he died. He was energetic, passionate, hilarious, ingenious, artistic, generous and full of love. He was 87 on October 27th when he died in his sleep at home in Escondido. This is not an obituary or a mournful tribute, but a small collection of memories I savor of a rare and significant contributor and curator of the Muscle Beach era and beyond.

George Eiferman introduced me to Russ in the summer of 1963. I have recalled the scene a hundred times since, thus reminding me of its personal importance, persuasion and delight.

A new recruit to the Weider California team (a team of three or four walking in circles and scratching our heads), I was yet to find permanent digs. There I lie, sprawled on the new mustard-colored foldout couch in the small 5th Street office of the fledgling West Coast Weider Barbell Company. George—ever-eager Mr. Universe—Eiferman nudged my mattress gently (George did everything gently) and apologized (George was always apologizing) for waking me so early on a Sunday morning.

"Dave, I want you to meet my friend, Russ Warner."

I rolled over and stretched and wrestled with disjointed sleep, self-consciousness, hunger, recognition of new surroundings, and the appropriate response to meeting a blurry yet smiley figure at the foot of my borrowed and subject-to-visitors bed. Russ was engaged in chuckling, observing and expressing himself with bouncy movements of the shoulders and arms.

"George, he looks like a corralled stallion being groomed for the next big race at Santa Anita. Let's sneak him a wild mare and run out the back door."

"Howdy, Mr. Warner. It's a pleasure to meet you, sir."

Within 10 minutes, we were ordering breakfast at Zucky's Deli on the corner, which was to become our favorite feeding trough over the amazing years to follow.

"I'll have a chicken-liver omelet, please, thank you." My favorite.

George was heading for Hawaii to open a gym, and Russ was taking his place as chief of the Weider West Coast operation. I was to spend the next three years with Russ to do what was needed to set Joe's muscle machine in motion. The road was long and uphill; the muscle machine was running on three cylinders, three wheels and a flat, but Russ could make clunky things go, and go fast.

Soon after dear George sought bluer skies and time did its maturing thing and greener grass began to grow beneath our feet, Russ uncovered his favorite gadget, tool and plaything, hobby, mode of artistic expression and master-key to the world of bodybuilding—his camera.

"Joe needs pictures for upcoming issues of the magazine, a few covers and some stories."

Russ was looking at the ceiling when he said this; there was no one else in the room.

"I'm the shipping clerk, Russ, the backroom guy."

I was looking at the floor when I said this.

"Yeah, I know," he agreed. "What are we going to do?"

By this time, I was scrutinizing the folder of 8x10s of Reg Park, Steve Reeves, Zabo, Clancy Ross, Jack Delinger and Jack LaLanne—my jaw dropped and with bulging eyes (typical expression of an east coaster during his first six months in California). The photos were a mixture of outdoor and studio shots in black and white, and with stark contrasts.

The men of sweeping muscle were the best, and the pictures exuded drama, inspiration and might.

"Shipping clerk" was still stuck in my throat.

Russ was twice my age, but he brought out the kid in me.

While I worried about the sky falling, Russ would tell me stories of Jack LaLanne walking down 10 flights of stairs on his hands or Clancy Ross and Jack Delinger performing feats of strength on Oakland street corners—things done with beer kegs and engine blocks and sledge hammers and always with a pretty neighborhood gal balancing atop their heads.

My scowl faded. Jersey's hard to shake, like the flu, maybe TB, poison oak…or barnacles.

Russ said, "There's a place I know in the Valley. The studios use it as a background for shooting westerns. They call it the Bat Crap Rocks. You'll love it; it's full of cool rock formations and desert and cactus. It's secluded. You and I and Dick Tyler can cruise out in a couple of weeks and shoot a few rolls of film…it'll be fun…a test run… no one will see them…just us…promise…I'll bring sandwiches… whadaya say?"

I, the backroom guy from Jersey, said almost inaudibly and without stirring conviction, "But, I…I'm not, well…gee-whiz…do I have to…sandwiches?…okay."

Nuts.

Russ posed my girth against some photogenic outcroppings, and the pictures ran in the magazines for an entire winter season. A magician of the lens with forbearance and gentle persuasion managed rocks and unwilling flesh into striking shots, making me feel a small part of the California landscape, the West Coast bodybuilding scene.

Once, when the shipping was complete and four tons of fresh free weight was unloaded from a Bobcat and neatly stacked in the backroom, Russ and I sat, fatigued and peaceful, in the inner office.

The radio was on softly and we talked about, who knows what—the freeway traffic, the weather, lunch—when the programming was interrupted to make an urgent announcement: President Kennedy had been shot while in Texas and was being rushed to a hospital. We were shocked side-by-side, Russ and I, and the magnitude of the raw horror overwhelmed us.

My older friend had served as a lieutenant in the Navy, as did JFK, understood politics, and was affected more quickly and more deeply than I. There was a strain in his face and I heard a solemnity in his voice, levels of disgust and disappointment I had not yet developed. We were in big trouble together and enduring a cataclysmic fate—a connection I didn't fully understand at the time.

A mutually endured catastrophe is bonding.

Where were you when JFK was shot? It's a strange question that arises now and then, and there I am with Russ in a dimly lit place listening to a small wood-veneer radio, gripped with reality. We locked the doors and went to Zucky's for coffee, fresh air, daylight and hope.

Then, later, "Yo, Dave, Joe needs pictures. I'll meet you at the Marina this afternoon after work."

But Russ, it's the middle of October and I don't have a tan and I'm 10 pounds overweight and it's freezing down there…and windy. Okay…

"Yo, Dave, Joe needs pictures. Let's shoot over to Century Boulevard in Century City and you can stand among the fountains and we'll get some great stuff."

Aw, Russ, it's the middle of March and I'm bulking up for a powerlifting challenge at Peanut's Westside Barbell Club and I haven't seen my trunks since we came back from the Marina.

Okay...

"Yo, Dave, Joe needs pictures. Let's go to my studio in the back of Vince's Gym. He wants indoor shots with heavy lighting."

Gee, Russ, I feel like a frog...and so forth and so on.

Russ just nodded and told me I looked great as he applied oil and adjusted the backdrop, lights, umbrellas, lenses and my attitude.

We laughed at what a pickle puss I was and he swore it was from too much tuna and water and not enough sex. At 21, I thought he was dirty ole man...but very funny.

When I was the Gladiator for KHJ-TV, Russ was my agent. He knew people in Hollywood and was well liked.

It turns out Mr. Warner was Jack LaLanne's trusty TV manager and producer and good friend. They trained at Muscle Beach in the '50s, and Russ practiced his photography while Jack practiced his hand balancing. Russ was behind the camera and by Jack's side while Jack was on-camera inspiring folks to get in shape and eat right.

I visited Russ's home one day somewhere near Pasadena—who knows where, he was driving—and when we pulled into his driveway, all I could see was a 60-foot antennae lashed down by thick cables protruding from his backyard. He was a king of the ham radio; one entire room was lined with dials, knobs and gauges, amplifiers, reducers, clusters of wires and speakers and microphones.

In front of the complex of communication equipment was a narrow runway with two or three stools with wheels to allow him to scoot about as he activated the gadgetry and spoke to friends across the world. He told me it was something he picked up in the Navy.

In his garage sat eight immaculately restored vehicles (my favorite a Cadillac Eldorado), which he claimed made his heart sing and kept him busy in his spare time.

The singing part I understood, but what spare time? This I have always pondered. How much can one guy do?

After Weider, one must get a real job for a while; it restoreth the soul and pays the accumulated bills. Russ went into the distribution of home gym equipment throughout central California and called his very successful venture All American Fitness. Missing show biz and loving bodybuilding, he introduced a popular, first-class physique show called The Russ Warner Classic, which ran thru the mid-'70s and '80s. I often sat in the front row or roamed around backstage, while my wife Laree expertly wielded her Nikon from the edge of the stage. We later had some cool shots of contenders from those days hanging on the walls of the World Gyms in Santa Cruz and Scotts Valley.

And so the story goes. Russ retired down San Diego way, and along with his buds, Leo Stern and Steve Reeves, put together some classy old-timers' gatherings. Old bodybuilders never die; they just keep on bombing and blasting and pushing that iron.

Russ Warner has a secret fan club and its members regularly bump into each other and exchange affectionate tales of Russ Warner at expos and contests and memorials, the latter becoming a frequent form of entertainment and gathering of good old friends. The membership was impressive and includes a lot of bright and shining stars; Gene Mozee, John Balik, Don Howorth, Dick Tyler, Larry Scott, Rosemary Hallum, Stern and Pearl, Bob Delmontique, the Tannys, the LaLannes, the Weiders…the list is as long as a Barry Bonds home run if he was on protein powder.

I love and respect and am supremely grateful for Russ.

Oh, wait. One more silly story.

Russ had one of those little colorful cylinders that when inverted would emit a mooing sound like a cow giving birth.

When we were all busily and quietly working at the little Weider shop—Russ, Ray Raridon, Annie (Joe's aunt), and I—and the silence was as thick as a cloud, Russ would turn over the little round cow-box and let 'er rip. He'd then come running out of his office on tip-toes like a mischievous child and huddle with Ray and me, as we cracked up with hands over our mouths to muffle and contain our laughter.

We called this hilarious.

We were grown and responsible men, well on our way to achievement, recognition and social contribution. The terrific, silly noise drove poor Annie nuts and, though we adored her, we submitted to the naughty joke. We figured Annie, who thought we were juvenile and who sat at the front counter representing The Weider Barbell Company to California and was four times older than Ray at 19 (76 years old and under five foot and 90 pounds), should have an extraordinary sense of humor. We were introducing her to such exceptional humor.

Russ said we were being sensitive. Where's that little round box full of laughs when you need it?

SEQUINS AND PEARLS

The weekend before the Mr. America contest in 1965, my training was going well, as far as I could tell. The truth was, I didn't yet know how to tell. I looked okay, but compared to what or whom? I was working hard, eating hard, braced with hard discipline and the abs were hard.

My first months at Muscle Beach were a crash course and I established training methods I was to follow forever. I quickly learned the essentials and settled into private, unmitigated early-morning workouts. They were silent, undistracted and unrelenting: no compromise and no competition. How sweet it is.

Two years of isolated training and I wasn't sure who I had become. I moved with three different training partners at different stages, and the reinforcement and friendships were priceless. They knew the Mr. A was on my mind, and they stood by my side; they were too close, however, to offer the critique and counsel I now sought.

Only an outsider could provide an evaluation and dare to place it in my hands. Who could I trust? I needed to know if I was ready for the competition in New York City only eight days away.

I also needed a pair of posing trunks.

Procrastination is one of my specialties, followed by irresponsibility and dimwittedness.

If you got on Washington Boulevard and followed it east for five miles, you'd find yourself in East Los Angeles and standing in front of Bill Pearl's Gym. If you walked in the front door at 6:00 pm, you'd find Bill, forearms pouring out of a cut-off sweatshirt, sitting behind a wood desk, chair tilted against the wall. If you arrived at 6:00 am, he was under a bar, bench pressing or squatting some absurd weight for a lot of reps. His training partners would be exuding energy, zeal and perspiration.

For my first visit, I chose the evening hour, after a gentlemanly phone call to assure he would be there. Bill was the man I could and would trust with the deed of critical analysis; thumbs up or…er… thumbs down.

A legend, Mr. Universe served in the Navy, built and owned several gyms over the years, Bill Pearl was known for his incredible power and ability to bend coins and tear license plates and phone books in half. Bill's accomplishments, when piled one on top of the other, present a towering skyline to my fields and fences. He's instructed NASA's astronauts in fitness, has five Mr. Universe trophies from different eras and continents stashed someplace safe, tours the world representing the biggest and best fitness corporations, and his wife, kids and friends love him. He owes no one and doesn't wear a watch.

The latter is the only semblance we have in common.

"Hi, I'm Dave. Can you tell me if I have muscles? I don't know."

"Sure, Dave. Why don't you come here tomorrow morning at six when my huge partners and I can stand you under the skylight and take a good look. Bring your posing trunks."

Me and my mouth. How could I say, "Never mind," or "I don't have posing trunks?"

There are the tough times, when you can't go forward and you can't go back and you can't lie. The only thing left was the truth. I was right on time, my big grin and my big gym bag and my big feet. I found the skylight on my own, but couldn't find my posing trunks. No problemo, Big D, you can borrow mine.

Bill's generosity is overwhelming. I didn't ask for music. The silence was loud enough.

I hit a few shots like Joe Weider, The Master Blaster, taught me. Joe could pose a molting ostrich and he'd win the overall and most muscular hands down at any pro show on the globe. The gold metallic trunks Bill offered fit perfectly and I felt pumped by the end of my routine.

The guys were excited and full of suggestions, which further warmed me up and briefly put the disabling self-consciousness to rest.

A few more run-throughs with additions and deletions, a change in timing and tempo, posture, facial expression and attitude adjustments, and I was a different animal.

"You can win this thing, Draper. I'm tellin' ya."

A PATH UNWINDING

After seeing a film clip after one of our IronOnline Bash events, I decided I should get a job on a farm. Baling hay, milking cows and shoveling manure can keep me in great shape, out of trouble and out of view. And it's good for the soul to put one's might into something worthwhile, earthy and productive.

I go to the gym with good intentions; they're always fulfilled, and I leave a better person for it. I also leave slightly beat up. I look back and recall it was that way 50 years ago when I emerged from the subterranean digs of the Muscle Beach gym too. It was barely daylight when I entered, and two or three hours later, milk was delivered, kids were in school and the hot sun was pouring from cloudless blue skies. Squinting, I staggered to my nearby car.

And the beat goes on. My life has virtually followed the same path ever since. Any day I expect a gold-plated watch from my boss at work with an engraving on the back saying, "Thanks for 40 years of dedicated service. We're proud of you."

Odd, because I don't have a boss and I don't work for anybody. Never did, not really. If I had have, I wouldn't have lasted 40 days, forget 40 years. Do this and do that from anyone but me is a little tricky. Either I get it wrong, or I don't listen, or both.

And what would I do with a watch? I can tell time, but I don't wear rings, trinkets, bobbles or beads. It's not that I don't admire the beauty of diamonds in settings of gold, or the sentiments behind them, but I don't need them…they're bothersome and costly. I don't even wear sunglasses or a wedding band.

No tattoos anywhere, come to think of it. I'm plain.

I once tied a piece of beige yarn around my neck for no particular reason during the summer of 1970. I forgot about it. How, you ask? Just look at my hair in those days and you'll notice I wasn't paying attention to personal details beyond muscle and might.

Later that year, I was looking at photos of me onstage in New York and London and there was this piece of yarn around my neck. How dumb is that? In one sweeping motion, I looked down (like I could see it?), and reached for my neck.

It was gone. Disintegrated, I suspect. For an instant, I felt naked.

I wore headbands for years, an ornament of sorts, but they were necessary gear to keep my shaggy hair out of my eyes. And the headbands were made of anything that was handy when the need arose—a strip torn from a towel, a cut from an old flannel shirt, a length of cord. Nothing snappy.

Bodybuilders in my day and my neck of the woods were poor. Those shredded Ts and sweatshirts that clung to our backs were all we had, not designer threads by Victorio's Secret Muscle Garments.

Material things were scorned in Venice in the '60s and '70s, which was good because none of us wanted to work, like at a real job, because our freedoms would be oppressed.

Freedom was another item of that era that was dealt with most unusually. So much freedom was sought by the free that the search almost became a prison itself. So in love with an illusion of freedom, we nearly kissed the real thing goodbye.

We all contributed to society, none of us were dropouts and were always engaged and prosperous in our own ways. There were school teachers, postal workers, a few engineers, a couple of landlords, a good-sized handful of studio employees—extras, stage crew, film and sound techs.

Zabo was the first personal trainer I ever met (1963). He was training 20 years before we met and trained until the day he died.

I asked Zabo, "What is the best exercise for biceps?"

We were buds for a long time, and went on various adventures near and far. The man was known for his simple wisdom, keen wit and adversity toward the ruins of ambition. He answered my provocative query in detail, "Curls."

I was not surprised.

I continued. "What is the best exercise for triceps...shoulders... chest...back... thighs...calves?"

He answered each question generously, patiently and in order: dips...front presses...incline presses...deadlifts...squats...donkeys.

"Anything to add?"

I was riveted.

"Yeah, train hard, don't miss, keep it basic and eat lots of chicken, fish, red meat and salads. Red wine won't hurt ya."

Some things never change.

The 13-odd-years in the center of my life—21 to 35—spent along the coast of LA stand out like a monument, an anchor and a millstone. Those years formed me, brought me up, taught me, stabilized me... and brought me down with a thud.

They took forever, and what a ride. My 21 years in Jersey by comparison are a child's blurry vacation, and my later years in northern California seem like a long weekend mixed with business and pleasure.

The beat goes on.

NOCTURNAL PROWESS

Darkness fell quickly that winter evening in southern Africa. Reg Park and I set out on our 50-mile journey through the countryside of Johannesburg to a village where physical culture was budding. No obstacles were foreseen; one makes a simple plan and simply executes it.

Shortly into our trek, only 10 miles out of town, our ride became an irregular bumping. The small vehicle affectionately nicknamed "Frenchy" rebelled, contorted and dragged us into a ditch. I, the designated driver (thinking it cool to be cruising the great Dark Continent with Reg Park, the lion and tiger of bodybuilding) was reduced to a struggling nitwit who found the nail that pierced the tire that pitched us into the precarious posture.

An early morning and engagements throughout the day promoting fitness to an uneducated audience left the two of us spent, somber and dull; show us the hoops and jump we will, but don't expect anything fancy or creative from this tattered pair.

We groaned, worked our way free of the Renault, stood up and watched the car rise once relieved of our bodyweight.

No cell phone; no AAA on-the-spot tow service, no highway patrol, no traffic on the two lane bi-way. Cozy. Reg, Hercules himself, looked at me. I, the Los Angeles Gladiator and Bomber from America, tempted to defensively whine, "I didn't see the nail," looked at Reg. He flexed his enormous calves. I clenched my fists.

We both shrugged our shoulders and grinned.

One of those flashlights the size of a pen hung from the key chain and broke the darkness to reveal a spare tire, a lug wrench and no jack. Without a word, we proceeded one step at a time, thinking that as each step was accomplished, the next would be revealed and its execution enabled. The logic was that of the modern-day muscleman, the only wisdom we understood: Action plus muscle equals solution.

We were partners and moved as one. Quickly, we memorized our surroundings, enabling us to pull the spare tire from the trunk and place it near its destination, the rumpled left-rear wheel. Our hands as feelers and our eyes now focusing out of need and will, we removed all the lugs but one. An occasional dash of light from the magic pen assured us of our perspective: tires, lugs, wrench and car position.

Now the next step was clear: Take off the troublesome flat tire, put on the trouble-free round tire.

Darkness is empowering. The absence of options contributes to might. No need to make decisions conserves energy for the action. The mystery of the black beyond our reach stimulates adrenalin, which heightens the senses.

Reg grabbed the bumper and gave it a few warm-up tugs as he set his footing aright. You need to realize we had worked out very early that morning, and heavy bench pressing was the subject. Our timing of "the spot" was impeccable.

Ready? One, two, lift.

The car went up, the wheel came off and was swept under the chassis as a support, and down came the car.

A dash of light renewed our viewpoint and positions. This time on the count of three, I lifted the left rear engine-bearing corner of Frenchy as Big Reg jammed the good wheel on and fed it the lugs.

He tightened them as I put the trunk in order. He insisted I drive and off we went, besmudged, but no worse for the effort.

STEVE REEVES

A door closed recently that I expected would remain open forever: Steve Reeves died and I didn't know him. I stood behind him backstage at an extravagant Dan Lurie contest in Manhattan somewhere off Times Square; he was being awarded a medal of honor and I was pumping up for the evening's exhibitions.

I declined, that night, several offers to meet the man, the star, the legend of *Hercules*.

He was tall, stately and handsomely dressed. What was he doing here?—I wondered, the occasion too slight for his presence. I was an oily, smelly and gritty gym rat, a slovenly and garish image in comparison. I was, also, busy. Another time, I thought.

The Golden Fleece slipped through my fingers.

I missed Steve Reeves on the silver screen as well. Though he gave majestic form to the meager goals I sought, he appeared to me only on posters. Movie-going was out of reach during my childhood.

The beauty and heroics of this *Hercules*, however, could not be chained.

I ached to look like him and knew I couldn't. It wasn't until after winning the Mr. America that I saw him again; television portrayed him in commercials through a 17-inch RCA. There was no hiding the handsomest of men who possessed muscular grace beyond compare.

Not many people I hung with knew Reeves. The Muscle Beach originals—Zabo, Joe Gold, Chuck Collras, Armand Tanny—all knew him, yet gave small insight into his life.

Rich tales were shared about every real and imagined character who walked the sands of Muscle Beach or served hard time in the Dungeon and those stories relived by the players as the curtain closed on that burnished era. About Reeves, though, no stories, no observations, not a clue.

In 1963, I dropped out of the sky like a lost bell-tower pigeon from Jersey. Russ Warner picked me up in Santa Monica and saw to the restoration and redirection of my wings. A jewel, Russ took the classic and most-prized photographs of Steve Reeves, standing atop the world and seeking the heavens.

No one comes close to Reeves in stirring the heart by way of muscle and might, balance and striking feature, bearing and countenance. Curious, though—Russ, in all his vividness and vitality, gave me no notion of the man, Steve Reeves.

I ask and can answer only one question: Who, after all these years, comes close?

No one.

One doesn't take perfection, should one perceive it, and improve upon it. You can only admire it and feel very, very good.

GEORGE EIFERMAN, A HEART OF GOLD

Mr. Philadelphia 1947

Mr. California 1948

Mr. America 1948

Mr. Universe 1962

Many years ago, I boarded an aircraft at La Guardia—I believe they had commercial jets back then—and made my lone and curious way to Los Angeles. My nose was pressed against the window for most of the flight as I absorbed my first flying experience in wonder. The other side of the clouds, the tiny-toy real world with its little cars and rooftops, soft patchworks of countryside, lonely stretches of a crinkled mountain range; the scenery appeared and receded in slow motion as I sat still in the hum.

"Coffee?"

"Huh? Sure."

That's the planet earth sliding by.

For five hours, we chased the sun, catching it finally over the Sierras, and sure enough, landed at LAX late on a Thursday night. Airport terminals in the middle of the night are bent-body, tired places where bleary people roam, out of sync, underfed and fading.

That night, George Eiferman stood at the arrival gate wearing a grin and a Hawaiian shirt, mighty forearms and grip hanging loosely from short sleeves.

"Hi, Dave, I'm George. Have a nice trip? Welcome to California. Here, let me carry your bag."

And so began my friendship with a man whose heart was bigger than the immense world over which I had just flown. Originals cannot be duplicated; they can only be admired. Amid conversation to suit the hour and the needs, we made our way to lovely Santa Monica and the famous Muscle House, a crash pad on the Pacific, for my first night's sleep.

I don't think so. There were a dozen guys in two rooms sprawled out and snoring, and none of them in the dim light look like they had muscles or a job. Perhaps I could sleep on the couch in Weider's small office, wake up early, have some breakfast and get to work.

Lord, I needed to be alone.

Weider's—Weider Barbell Co.—was the small, sputtering West Coast branch of Joe Weider's yet-to-develop empire of muscles, magazines, pro contests, health food products and other related enterprises. George was sort of in charge of the two-month-old project, and I was imported from the Union City Headquarters to assist.

Two muscleheads to install one light bulb and it took us all day.

I took one look at Santa Monica in the morning summer sun and thought I was in heaven. George, the current Mr. Universe, and I, the current Mr. New Jersey, bumped around and got things done. Ann, Joe's aunt three times my age, kept a tender eye on George and me as she opened the mail and did the bookkeeping. A staff of three, rubbing sticks together.

Naturally, the first piece of business the day after I arrived was to settle into a workout. George took me to The Muscle Beach Gym three blocks southwest of my new digs and 30 steps down into the dark. Once my eyes and nose adjusted, I realized the dank and impoverished gym with all the amenities of a dungeon was my kind of place.

I met Wes and Zabo and Joe Gold and Chuck Collras and Marjanian and Artie Zeller and Hugo Labra and Peanuts West, and George benched 405 cold.

I benched half that and got splinters.

The summer smiled and my big friend showed me how to hang out at the beach and get rays and body surf like a log. It was during a such convulsive day in the waves that I collided with a long submerged and swollen body, the man who earlier had gone off a nearby pier.

I pushed, pulled and dragged him to shore and, exhausted, collapsed by his side. George observed my frenzied antics from a distance and, like a rhino, crossed the sand to my aid. Too late for either of us, the Pennsylvania transplant stood over me and commented with great enthusiasm, "This stuff only happens in California."

I nodded. He was right.

In September, we drove south to San Diego in George's 1955 Buick Special to present a show at a junior college. I'm wondering why a Mr. Universe titleholder is driving around in a beat-up old clunker, but don't say anything because I think it means he's poor. It wasn't very long before I learned that all titleholders are poor.

Under the lights of the small auditorium, George introduced the eager contestants of the local competition to the eager local audience.

Midway through the event, he invites a pretty volunteer from the second row to help him in a musical number. He begs, she concedes; he breaks out a dented but shiny trumpet as she looks on, waiting for a cue. He blurts out an off-key and vaguely familiar tune no one can identify; she waits for a clue.

Somehow, amid laughter and the blaring horn, the girl is suddenly up and over his head in a one-arm press. She's startled and George is doing his famous trick, parading around the stage in circles, accompanied by the mad tune and the screaming student.

I'm offstage trying to pump up because I'm next with my corny posing routine. How am I ever going to follow this act?

Ralph Kroeger, a popular gym owner in a nearby community, demonstrated with precision the three Olympic lifts performed in the 1960s. Eventually, Jack Lalanne got hold of the mic and raised the revolutions with his passion for health and fitness. Somebody gave out trophies and everyone went home. The Buick pulled into Santa Monica around midnight without overheating.

Two weeks later, George was to introduce me to a wonderful man with a camera, Russ Warner, my new boss. Seems Mr. Eiferman was moving to Hawaii with his bride to open a gym. Didn't see him much after that. We both wandered this way and that; later, he opened a successful gym in Las Vegas in the 1970s.

He died there after complications that often accompany people nearing 80 years old.

A most unforgettable man, he had a heart of gold, strength of an ox, a corny sense of humor honed to perfection, the disposition of a muscle-building saint, humility of a '55 Buick and color of a Hawaiian shirt, loyalty of a Golden Retriever and faith and wisdom apportioned by God.

STEEL-WINGED WARRIORS, IRON-FEATHERED FRIENDS

Last week, we zipped down the coast to Venice Beach for the 4th of July, where the zillionth annual Mr. and Miss Muscle Beach contest was held. We sat amid hundreds of enthusiastic beach, body and sun worshippers cheering this year's crop of natural musclebuilders from the Venice Muscle Beach Gym and other close-by facilities.

The day was perfect Southern California; Venice was hopping the way only Venice can hop—up, down and sideways, in circles and loops of various descriptions, suddenly and at once—and the tan and gleaming competitors were smiling broadly. The contest was held on the beach at the beautifully upgraded lifting platform and staging area.

The judges sweated as they worked hard in the hot sun; the spectators encouraged every colorful moment; the muscular guest posers stunned onlookers and the show was pitched with spirited intensity by a popular Mr. America from the good old days, Bill Grant, the Master of Ceremonies.

Bill and I trained side by side at Joe Gold's gym, the original, real-deal Gold's Gym on Pacific Avenue (circa '63–73), home of the champions before the microwave and cell phones, and today share the secrets of getting huge and ripped with anyone who'll listen.

Few people love and understand the sport of muscle-building as much as Bill Grant, and his integrity is always evident. The man is ripped, fun and funny and I don't hate him even a little because of it. He's also about five years younger than me and has all his hair, and it's there that I draw a line in the sand.

An awesome fitness entrepreneur, Joe Wheatley, promoted the show in conjunction with the Venice Parks and Rec. The whole affair, which continues to this day, is a promising reflection of one community getting behind physical culture, a healthy and grateful page from the past pasted in today's sparse fitness scrapbook. Let's see more readiness and less laziness, more muscle and less fat, more strength and less weakness, more courage and less fear, more discipline and less disorder and more spirit and less languor.

Let's rock 'n' roll with the iron 'n' steel.

There, I was presented the Muscle Beach Hall of Fame award, and of course I am not the slightest bit proud, humility along with charm and bounteousness being among my finer features. I also received the Spirit of Muscle Beach award in July of '99 from Bill Howard, grand-master muscleman and forefather of Muscle Beach, and presenter of the famous contest for 37 years.

You can shake my hand now or at the end of this bit.

After the event, we walked with what seemed like the rest of LA to the boat-filled channel of nearby Marina del Rey. Did I say nearby? We walked until our legs unscrewed, one by one. There was a fireworks display and the spirit of freedom surrounded us. Kaboom, spray, sparkle, glitter, kaboom, boom, red, green and blue flashes, crack, crack, hiss, bang and pop. Walking back was a fierce challenge, with the calves and upper quads begging for mercy.

Speaking of quads, the police were in four-packs on foot, on bikes and in cruisers. No dope, no booze, no jerks, no problem. Everyone was up and nobody went down.

There's more, but I'll be brief. On Monday, the following morning, we visited the World Gym headquarters in Marina Del Rey and hung with Eddie Giuliani and Zabo and, to my surprise, Dick Dubois, a 1950s Mr. America star. I hadn't seen Dick since my arrival in

California over 50 years ago. He was looking as vigorous, strong and rugged as ever. He was a good man who preached the Good Word in a small bible-teaching church in Santa Monica and lifted weights religiously, a long haul from his Mae West days in Las Vegas with Zabo and The Gold.

Good to talk with the boys and soak up the latest noise.

I gabbed with Joe for an hour about this and that and we wondered how much weight we'd lifted in our lifetimes.

"Makes me weary thinking about it, Drapes," he said, as I said, "Goodbye, Joe."

Heading out of town, we took a short impromptu detour through the San Fernando Valley. Leroy Colbert's Total Nutrition Center at the time was on the corner of any street and Ventura Blvd in Sherman Oaks. Saying hello to Leroy was always an inspiring and glad time and as we pulled into the parking lot, lo and behold, it was Bill Grant wedging his car next to ours.

Coincidences always make me wonder. The four of us were sharing our disbelief walking to the store's entrance when who's that trotting down Ventura but Shawn Perine. Just the day before, we all sat together on the hot sand, rapping, discovering, planning, rooting, applauding and eventually bidding farewell.

It's getting stranger by the minute…restless clouds are bristling overhead and we await the thunder from on high. Bubbling through the door at once, we five large kids find Big Leroy beaming with open arms, like he knew we were coming.

It's time for hugs, handshakes, slaps on backs and hours of conversation about the sameness and difference of things, what's come, gone and about to be, how time flies and how lucky we are.

SO LONG TO THE GOLD

Joe Gold died the week after the Muscle Beach Hall of Fame trip. He was 82 years old; heart complications earlier this year initiated a general downslide in his well being. He was active with projects until the end, and recognized death as a place where he'd be "reunited with old friends."

He was a tough guy, an authority figure, straight as an arrow piercing a bull's eye. He built his first Gold's gym in Venice with his own hands and the hands of his buddies. You know the place; it's where the Golden Era of bodybuilding was conceived and its rambunctious brats grew big and strong.

The cinderblock workshop on Pacific Avenue was decked with muscle-building equipment of thick iron engineered and constructed by Joe Gold himself and amused and comforted a rare family of brothers. Artie Zeller, bodybuilding's Van Gough with a Roloflex, composed inspirational portraits of the brawny gang as they restlessly played amid steel muscle-building contraptions, indestructible benches and superior pulley systems.

There's a series of black and white photos taken in the summer of 1970 with Frank Zane, Franco, Katz, Arnold, Waller, Zabo and me barging about Joe's upgraded, second-generation, ground-level dungeon. Bare stone walls and smooth-running heavy-metal torture racks stimulate and induce hard training and muscle growth. You can hear the weights rattle and clang as they're loaded on bars; you can feel the strain of sinew and might under hot resistance and you understand muscular satisfaction with every strenuous exhale.

The pictures speak, they tell the story.

From that gnarly gym—the original among imitations—grew a large population of World Gyms, a non-pushy, responsible and respectful gym licensing company where fewer jerks and more cool people gather.

Running a gym is not a laughing matter, I discovered in our endeavors, and when confronted with an unknown I'd ask myself, "What would Joe do?" An unknown was, in fact, anything and everything, including the layout of the gym equipment, the collection of past dues, breaking up a fight, implementing rules and regulations, asking troublemakers to leave and maintaining respect and responsibility.

What am I, a cop?

"To keep it simple," Joe said, "run your gym like you run your house. Keep it clean and in good running order. No jerks allowed, members pay on time and if they give you any crap, throw them out. There's peace where there's order."

The gym became a sound refuge for many; it paid its bills and made no money, it sparkled, displayed no graffiti or broken windows and there wasn't a jerk in sight. All the troublemakers made their way to the gyms down the street or the next town over, where they were typical, packed jungles. Integrity before the dollar is worth a fortune.

Because of his authentic Muscle Beach-ness and Mae West days in Las Vegas, his innovative gym equipment design and gym-empire building, his generosity to the underdog, honesty, commonsense and worldly courage and stoicism, The Gold became good and important to many people. He was an icon in the subculture of bodybuilding and physical culture.

Only the folks who trained in his gym knew that for 25 years, he didn't let Big Bill Pettis from Pennsylvania go hungry, unclothed or unsheltered, when almost anyone else would have chased him away with a stick.

An anonymous giver, Joe took Arnold under his wing when the young lad from Austria first arrived in California. If you were visiting from out of town and wanted a workout, the place was yours. He gave me woodworking projects when I was down and out, and paid me in advance so I could eat.

Zabo, Eddie Giuliani, Steve Cepello, Mike Uretz and Arnold would gladly take the microphone from my hand and tell stories of Joe's armor-plated character and fighting spirit. Those who sailed with him during the years he toured as a merchant marine said the ships' captains came to rely on his steadfastness.

Joe could poke fun at life without meanness or disrespect and had name for everybody shaped by their nature and mannerisms: The Chief, Nature Boy, 911, Bug Eyes, Slick Dick, XR, The Fish, Doctor Strangelove, The Good Wife, Cyclops.

He took risks when everyone else took shelter. He took aim when others took flight. He walked, hiked and trudged when others stumbled or pulled up lame. They simply don't make them like that anymore. His broad smile lit up a room.

Sometime in 1967—spring, I think—the Muscle Beach Dungeon was losing ground at its subterranean digs. It was then that I pulled up stakes and moved to Joe's facility to carry on my training. Mr. America and Mr. Universe were behind me and the continuation of bodybuilding as a competitive sport and the primary motivator in my life was questionable.

There I sat in Joe's gym on that first day. It was early morning and the sun was blazing through the huge translucent windows facing Pacific Avenue in Venice. I hadn't seen the sunlight this time of day for years, my customary position in The Dungeon being at least 20 feet below ground level. I felt self conscious, almost naked, and I noticed the rags on my back were exactly that: rags on my back. I could see this for the first time because there were mirrors on the walls the size of billboards.

Who's the creature? What kind of place is this? I felt as if I'd been extracted from my private and primal world against my will. I don't need no stinking mirror to look at myself.

What's that, I hear voices! It sounds like people. There are no shadows, no dark corners, no place out of plain view. They'll see me if I don't do something quick.

I buried myself under a bench press. Works every time.

Once I got past the sunlight, mirrors, half-dozen morning people, fresh air and sense of the living and breathing, things really kicked in. Like, there were these incredible cable systems with real pulleys six inches in diameter for smooth-rolling action, not the kind of rope pulleys we had before, the kind used for drying underwear in the backyard.

There were rugged steel benches instead of colossal splintery wood structures, Olympic bars that weren't bent like trailer truck springs, and dumbbells that were balanced and machine bolted, not welded one drowsy afternoon in some beefy tan guy's driveway.

I felt modern, slightly spoiled and feared I'd get soft, but soon realized gravity is gravity and might is might.

Besides, all these contemporary conveniences bore the Joe Gold signature and they were guaranteed to build big muscles practically overnight. No one made the claim, but I could tell by the way they felt: Just right.

Old bombers never die, they just fly away. If you see an airborne craft on the horizon tipping its wings, it's probably The Gold saying, "Press on."

Joe was honored at a grand memorial held in Marina Del Rey a few weeks later. The Del Rey Yacht Club was packed with friends from all walks of life who were invited (and requested not to wear jeans, tank tops and flip-flops). Half the crowd grumbled and had some shopping to do before the event, including me, but anything for Joe.

There was an open bar and a swell assortment of food to pile on plates, but folks were much too busy catching up on old times with old friends who had vanished over the years. There were originals from Muscle Beach who balanced on each other's shoulders when the sun was brighter and the air clearer and the streets less congested.

A mic was passed around and Jack Lalanne praised Joe for his hard work; Joe Weider spoke of his exercise equipment contributions and promised a beefy article on The Gold in an upcoming issue of *Muscle and Fitness;* Mickey Hargitay of Tarzan and the Mae West show told nostalgic stories; Frank Zane drew upon his harmonica and song writing to compliment Joe; Bill Pearl said he was a tough and true leader who never sought attention, and Arnold pointed to Joe's generosity and warm nature hidden beneath a thorny rosebush.

We shared the affair with Dick Tyler, writer, chiropractor and Muscle Beach original currently best known for his book, *West Coast Bodybuilding Scene*—the most historical and lovable and readable insight into the Golden Era of bodybuilding. We laughed with and at each other as we wallowed in the rare and rich collection of living musclehood memorabilia.

There's big Lou Ferrigno on crutches and there, Tom Platz. Is that Harold Zinkin and Leo Stern? Leroy Colbert, over here, it's Draper. Heads bobbed, bodies bowed, people embraced, laughter rose and hands shook in handshakes.

Life's a slice.

GEORGE BUTLER, GOING BACK

Going back to rummage through my mind can be a musty experience. Not every thought I turn over is a precious and delicate item of nostalgia, or a rusty and rugged tool used to forge a splendid future. Dim recollections, they're more like sagging, threadbare, spring-popping mattresses and worn-out, tight-legged bell-bottoms: often embarrassing, uncomfortable and tiresome.

The 1970s were for me lusterless and without grand imagination—not necessarily bad years, they just happened.

What went on in the land of bodybuilding, I'm not sure. I carried on my merry weight lifting with internal enthusiasm and fulfillment like a fisherman in a secret cove on his favorite lake. I missed the Olympias, the Mike Mentzer-Arnold Schwarzenegger battle and the whole muscle population explosion. It's as if I had peacefully slept.

One day amid those sleepy times, Artie Zeller came to my house in Playa Del Rey for a friendly visit, as he often did to break up his day. This time, he brought with him a nice young man, George Butler; both men were carrying large, professional cameras.

I was working on a chandelier of beams, chain and rusted iron the size of a Volkswagen. The torch was blazing and tools were scattered everywhere in my workplace.

I looked like...well...a madman: broken goggles, shredded jeans, barefoot and generally dirty.

I had taken up heavy barbell curls and push-presses for the summer and was busting out of a tie-dyed tank top.

This pleasant scene was further enhanced by my bearing the lingering symptom of mild acetylene poisoning: a slack, slightly paralyzed jaw.

Conversation was one-sided. I listened and uttered grunts as we sat around that enlightening afternoon: George Butler, a smooth gentleman, the *Pumping Iron* film master, and me, the Bomber gone bonkers.

You can't live and die by your horrific faux pas. They're indelible and cring-worthy, yet so outrageous as to be too good to be bad. To this day, I smile at thought of the day and am flattered by the visit. You can't kill pride.

And for all these years, I thought the good fellow thinks I'm a nut. Wait. The story has just begun.

Pumping Iron, the film that breathed super life into bodybuilding and set it among the constellations, celebrated its 25th anniversary in the spring of 2000. The writer, producer and director, George Butler, was at the Arnold Classic, also celebrating its 25th year in Columbus.

In conjunction with Arnold's big show, a gathering of the film's stars—Franco, Lou, Arnold, Ed Corney, Mike Katz—were being interviewed for an HBO special as part of the film's re-release that summer—a staggering coincidence in the year 2000.

A further coincidence, as a spokesman for World Gym, I was also there, and wondered if I'd bump into George. Now that I could speak, I could, no doubt, put my entire foot in my mouth.

Friday, late morning as a World Gym convention breakfast was winding down, I was invited to the stage to welcome the gym owners to the seminars that were to follow. As I approached the microphone, a special acknowledgement was made to a celebrity in the audience: *Pumping Iron's* own, George Butler. Evidence of his reverence was clear.

I slurped out a few heart-felt words...hi, nice, good, happy, er, swell, so-long...and casually made for the famous exit, where George stood beaming with both hands extended.

One looking on might think we were long-lost friends. As, indeed, we were.

The obvious next thing long-lost friends must do is to get to know each other. As we were off in different directions for the day, we arranged an appointment for a half-hour interview later that evening. Instead, the interview went on for nearly two hours during which we recorded historical gaps and recent enterprises.

No mention was made of the elaborate hanging lamp of burned beam and rusted metal or the clown that hung it 25 years ago.

Upon parting George put his hand to his heart and said, “You bury me or I’ll bury you.”

Friends for life.

I grabbed the down elevator to hustle me to my room, and as I assumed a position at the rear, a chorus of voices beamed my name. It was Reg Park and his lovely wife, Marion, dressed in formal black as they headed for The Arnold Classic main event.

We hugged and jabbered until the elevator dumped us in the lobby. It had been 30 years since the three of us stood together, their home in Johannesburg being our last rendezvous in the spring of 1969 when Reg and I did shows together to promote his gyms in Africa from Salisbury to Cape Town.

Time does not fly, but it does march on.

TRAVELS WITH ZANE

Embarrassment—we nearly give up life, liberty and limb to avoid this wretched exposure of our raw and delicate ego. Also known as humiliation, this cruelest of feelings is something I endure regularly and find extraordinarily educational. Kind of like a training injury; it gets your attention, causes you to focus and guides you on to repair and rehabilitation.

Hopefully, it makes you a stronger person.

I have one such memory that's clear and still causes me to shudder.

Frank Zane, his dear wife Christine and I met at the Paris Central Train Station at 7:00 one downcast autumn morning to continue our tour of Europe. It was a busy mid-week workday and Europeans use the rails like we use our precious cars to get around; up-town, cross-town, and out of the country.

We were destined to arrive in Brugge, Belgium, by early afternoon. Our express was packed with solemn commuters subject to another day of mundane travel, newspaper folded, thermos underarm, briefcase in hand.

As if in a black and white segment of life, we ever so slowly lurched forward: the collective metal of 17 passenger cars and freight carriers creaked and groaned.

I looked across endless acres of track, side by side and intertwined, a scattering of switching poles and signal towers, distant corrugated factories, bleak and gray. There were engines of crushing size and power moving incredible mass and solid iron, with impossibly thick wheels and axles of steel. Smoke and steam idly drifted and belched from the leaky, Gothic landscape.

Frank looked uneasy, Christine smiled agreeably (everything about Christine is agreeable), and I sought to capture the moment. The London Mr. Universe was behind us, a rather sloppy performance on my part. I got a late start, grabbed the wrong bottle backstage and wound up smearing wheat germ oil on myself. Thick, gooey stuff like glue that smelled rancid got a lot of attention.

I barely got through that night—and that's not even "the embarrassment."

I'm using lighter fluid to remove the organic oil as the celebrations begin. Don't come near me with that match. Frank won the amateur Mr. Universe; Arnold, the pro Mr. Universe, and I came in third, after Reg Park.

The next day, I made a quick return to Ohio for an Olympia sortie with Arnold and Sergio Oliva, another hysterical blitz. And now, here I am with the Zanes for a brisk tour of Europe—just to say we did—and back to New York City for the Mr. Universe, Mr. America, Mr. World competitions.

Give me the "here and now," win or lose. I began to settle down to see what I could see. Soon we'd be traversing the romantic countryside of France, the sights and sounds of a very different place, perspectives of very different people.

Frank suddenly raised his window and stuck his head out as if he knew where we were and where we were going. The clanging, shiny and angular abstract of tracks told me nothing. Frank declared we were on the wrong train, going in the wrong direction. Christine's smile broke into something like laughter, and my sweet reverie bristled to alarm.

We conferred like the Three Stooges as our fellow commuters mildly looked on, entertained: Americans, a troublesome yet comical lot. They act as if their pants are on fire. Wish they'd stay home.

The train picked up speed; the clacking increased and the dense railway yard thinned out.

Frank, AKA Mr. Universe, leaped over me, hit the center aisle and in two strides, reached the box marked "Emergency Only." He shattered its glass with the tiny hammer and pulled the handle with the thrust of a heavy one-arm lat row. The train screeched as if tortured, all wheels locked and inestimable tons of mechanized iron slid to a pronounced halt.

The side door unlatched and partially opened, our escape.

Once stopped, we dragged the door open. At a time like this, you pretend nobody else exists, just you and your two invincible buddies. If only we could stop time, step out of the picture and watch from a safe place as the action resumed. We all looked down to discover we were six feet from the tracks and 500 yards from the station.

The commotion behind us was building and beginning to organize. As if catapulted by an unseen force, Frank and I were airborne with Christine close behind, still genuinely enjoying herself.

Heads were out the windows, hundreds of them. Necks straining, expressions of shock, fright, confusion, anger and relief. Hundreds of animated faces were shouting and glaring at us.

With no composure, no grace and no brains, we grabbed our luggage and made a run for it. You can probably picture this sad and desperate trio staggering as we balanced suitcases and gym bags over slick tracks and railroad ties with conductors, security police and a half-dozen furious passengers in hot pursuit.

Tell me I'm dreaming.

Frank did it. It was him.

I was tired and not up to the long walk back to the station. The conductors were prompt and serious. So were the police.

By the time we reached the concrete loading ramp, a sizeable crowed had gathered, and not a single person asked for an autograph or a most muscular pose. Instead, there was an interrogation through an interpreter, phone calls, paperwork, apologies, a fine…and we were in Brugge by early evening, gazing at the gentle old Europe of cobblestone streets and tiny backyards where gates hung crookedly on rusting hinges.

There, we received awards for our contributions to physical culture. My award was engraved on a six-inch brass plate; Frank's was a gold cup on black marble standing 18 inches tall.

I should have pulled the emergency cord. You see, it's that kind of directness and determination and oneness of purpose that enables one to win Mr. Olympia three times in a row.

IRON ONLINE LAS VEGAS STYLE

One moment you're speeding across a colorless and barren desert, the next you're standing awash in dazzling lights, sounds and sensations too plentiful to digest, and soon you're again competing for space on a strand of remote, bushy highway as if life was a race to the end. We live in the anticipation and preparation of the moments before us, and in the memory of the moments gone by. The occasion of the real thing—the moment itself—is seldom part of our experience; that is, unless the "real thing" is extraordinarily intense and the physics of living as we know it is transcended.

This Las Vegas IronOnline Bash trip delivered never a dull moment, no stress larger than a hiccup, no catastrophes, no regretful occurrences, no losses, if-onlys or could-haves. It was a rare combination of uncommonly nice and good and interesting people sharing a life-binding thread of time together and enjoying something worthwhile, pursuing the joys of health, muscle and might amid the struggle of living day by day.

The desert weather was perfect: clear, dry, sunny and agreeably hot days, followed by warm, sharply moonlit nights. Las Vegas offers her cornucopia of fruits and treats, both wholesome and forbidden, from sunrise to sunrise. Chance is in every sparkling casino; risk in the shadows of the sexy bars, easy trouble in dark corners if you're looking for it, and endless distractions around every curve and angle.

Mostly you feel safe and sound wherever you venture. Outdoors and in, you are on the move, whether standing still or cascading with the flood of animated and chattering pleasure-seekers of the world.

Not everyone is loose, energized and getting high. Boredom hollows the spirit, fatigue bends the back and world stress creases the faces of the workers attending the broad and insatiable appetites of the visitors. They live beyond the limits of the Las Vegas we know and separate themselves from the scene when each shift ends.

What attracts and entertains us; what is novel, extravagant and awesome to you and me is a routine they try to forget when the whistle blows and they clock out. It's not their party. The casino, the backstage, the restaurant and the taxi are jobs that pay the bills and permit the ebb and flow of daily living in desert suburbia.

Las Vegas has a monster-sized appetite. The energy needs of the city I see pulsating at night from the view of my 22nd floor perch are unfathomable: lights by the billions, air conditioning for millions of cubic feet of hot space, slots for a million armed bandits, elevators, escalators, loud speakers, special effects, alarm systems, hot water, stoves, refrigerators, microwaves, TVs, computers and on and on and on.

Sacks of money in well-protected piles lay everywhere like sandbags to stay the floodwaters of currency. The dice roll, the ball spins, the cards shuffle and hands are dealt. The house wins a lot, and a lucky few go home with a handful. Some folks don't go home at all.

A feast to feed the beast: Drinks, smokes and all-you-can-eat buffets satisfy the hunger of the partygoers and add to their disguised grief. A lot of cleavage, young and old, not frequently seen in hometowns, is on display on the runway.

I walked to a low sidewall of a cashier booth to peer at the machines processing the chips, cash and coins, and was instantly triangulated by three security men, their monotonous stares a warning that cameras everywhere were onto my agenda, innocent or otherwise. I withdrew like a professional, flexing my lats and inflating my chest. The three men cowered, then vanished, I'll bet a penny.

Forty-thousand square feet of Gold's Gym swallowed up a dozen brazen IronOnliners determined to share the heavy metal a thousand miles from home. They went in the mornings to gird themselves for the day and at night to quench a thirst we all know so well. Friday at 9:00 pm, while the city rocked and rolled, three dozen of us met in front of the gym to contemplate training, opting instead to confer, converse, relate, share and otherwise hang out and rub triceps and biceps at the juice bar. One by one, the crowd of sort-of-strangers became a gathering of familiar friends.

"Awkward" is the word that too often defines the scenes of adults collecting where a keg or bar is not somewhere in its midst, but that day, the weather or a silence did not once enter the spontaneous conversations bouncing off the walls. Jabber, hugs, laughter, old and new stories and camera flashes accompanied and propelled the grinning participants in circles. By 11:00, normalcy returned to the gym and the weight floor resumed its quiet Friday night appearance.

We then fled to the Strip to absorb and contribute a fair amount of energy, each of us glad we weren't in the line-up for the following day's competition. The Mr. Olympia would have to do without our ripped and tanned bodies this year.

Ever been to a business expo where retail items and products are on display by manufacturers or designers or distributors: computers or guns or boats or RVs or outdoors camping and sporting gear? Booths of differing dimensions and display-appeal cluster over thousands and thousands of square feet of open floor space, each represented by an articulate spokesperson or team of professionals. Buy and sell is the name of the game. Network and exchange is a positive alternative. What's new, tried and true, who makes it, where can you get it and for how much, are the questions asked and answered with savvy and finesse.

Yeah, right.

You walk into the Olympia Expo Hall and are promptly assaulted by a billion decibels of sound; yelling and hard music, heavy on the drums. Confusion is immediate and semi-permanent. The folks aren't milling about reviewing the goods and asking questions and making observations.

First of all, there are no folks; these are mostly bizarre characters, and no one mills about or asks anything. They intensely fight for their precious space as they're crushed by one another in a desperate attempt to traverse the length of the jammed aisles, leading to further pandemonium. If they're not hollering at one another, they are screaming or yelping.

The professionals have lumps on all parts of their partially clothed physiques. Half of them are men.

Dark tattoos are popular on top of the lumps, as are lumps on top of the lumps. I've never seen so much muscle-like skin in all my life. Skulls and cross bones seem to be trending, hanging from ears and neck chains and bracelets. Quickly, it's clear that this no peace rally. The mob seems like a good mob; only "I'm tough and bad" has gotten lodged somewhere in their unoriginal brains.

It's a little weird for those who had taken the road less traveled. It seems they missed the turnoff a few miles back.

Take me to my padded hotel room.

Later that afternoon, 150 enthusiastic faces sat before Frank Zane and me in the pleasant shade of the small pavilion, as the world's greatest caterers lovingly tended smoky fires and simmering foods. Speakers carried our voices, answers in response to questions that have been tricking all of us over the years of rattling the iron.

Both Frank and I were 60 years of age, with only months separating us, and our training techniques run parallel as train tracks traversing

America from east to west. When we approach a mountain or a river, we each assess the obstacle according to our industry and surmount it according to our resources. The destination is reached, though the routes he and I choose are different enough to offer passage to anyone heading in our direction.

The information is not in the answer, so much as it is in the answering.

We said little that was revealing or earth shaking, but our voices spoke of weight training and smart eating decades years in the making. Frank had to zoom to another Olympia weekend engagement; the food was ready for consumption, and I settled in to respond to several dozen flashing cameras and a final round of handshakes, questions and gratitude.

Thank you and you are welcome.

Within a few adrenalin-packed hours, the hall at the Mandalay Bay would be alive with oiled, pumped and heaving madness: competitors, judges and spectators in unison and at odds. Showtime at the Mr. O.

I'm told, a great show thrilled the participants...until the announcement of the winners and losers. Then, the disapproving audience lost its composure, entirely. No one was in the mood for politics or favoritism or contradiction to popular opinion, it seems, and though the contestants were toe-to-toe and shoulder-to-shoulder, the crowd saw it differently than the judges. In five minutes, the Olympia disintegrated into boos, walkouts and the tossing of objects.

And there you have it: the art, the passion, the sport and the love of bodybuilding during a Las Vegas weekend.

ARNOLD, THE GREAT

Over the years, it was not infrequently suggested that I open a gym, do what I like to do and live happily ever after. How did I know there was more to it than that?

The dumb idea was never remotely entertained, not even for a second. Enter one ear, exit the other. Goodbye.

One couldn't separate me from my training and the gym, but I cannot say it was a swell love affair that had me enthralled and blinded to other stimuli in life. I was not soaked in passion for barbells; my grip on the dumbbells was not a tender and longing embrace. I walked into the gym, nodded to anyone who was there and got to work, post haste. When the deed was done, I was gone.

One day a gym in town shuttered, and someone said, "Let's reopen it." I felt a little tug. Sounds simple enough. I mentioned it to Laree and the next day she was working on a business proposal. The following year we and our partners had a World Gym in Santa Cruz. October was the month, 1989 the year as we endured the earthquake that knocked central California silly.

Arnold watched the gym-building progress and said, "Dave, when you do a grand opening, let me know. I will help."

The gym was open for business, but the detail work was not complete until February the following year. Arnold's secretary called one Thursday afternoon: "Arnold has Friday a week from tomorrow free if you can put something together."

That great news for a grand opening could not have had better timing. We were dazed and stumbling seven days a week, sunrise to sunset—the tunnel with no end, not even an oncoming train in sight.

We leaped as if charged with electricity. In seven days, the tasks that had taken on the rigidness of road kill were completed. The word was out and newspapers and TV suddenly took interest in our project. Press releases were distributed and 30-second spots on local radio could be heard at prime times throughout the week.

Over a thousand people showed up with special passes that allowed entrance to the spectacular affair. Santa Cruz enjoys good food and the caterers were excited to oblige. Our little gym of 7,000 square feet was pleasantly over-run with extraordinarily well-behaved people.

There's a small, busy airport in neighboring Watsonville that's seen a jet or two in its past. Arnold and his entourage landed there, on time, no hitch, with the California Highway Patrol on hand to escort our white limousine convoy. It was extraordinary, driving up Highway 1 in two limos flanked by two motorcycles, another patrol car bringing up the rear.

What did the commuters think, I wonder.

Arnold and I talked about old times and skiing during the 30-minute drive. More than once, I felt like scrambling through the sunroof, shouting and waving at everybody. I fought the urge.

The crowd at the gym was still forming when we arrived at twilight. Arnold knew the work before him and immediately assumed his role. He penetrated the throng and began making his way through the gym, shaking hands, signing autographs and engaged in honest conversation with every opportunity as cameras clicked. At one point, he choreographed a group picture starring the local Special Olympics Team who gathered on the lifting platform in their colors and gear.

The hungry news media had a picnic. Conan the Barbarian, with Grace Jones and Sven-Ole Thorsen at his side, was laughing and playing and eating and drinking…live in Santa Cruz. The Terminator was stomping around in their backyard. Seven-time Mr. Olympia leaned against a squat rack and talked toward their cameras about muscles, politics and being a dad.

Never stalled for long, the big friendly guy made his way up the staircase to the loft where the cardio equipment spread out and another hundred people jammed for a birds-eye view of the action. The heat was building and the natives were getting restless; they began to grab at him and I knew the end was near.

I joined Arnold, now with Joe Gold, to act as the host and his right guard, Joe on his left. We made our way to the steel railing and looked down at the ebullient fun-makers, a mass of mild and congenial rioters. It was my turn to speak to them, thank them and introduce them to the evening's mystery guest. But how could I expect to gain their attention? How could I dare interrupt the frolic?

Er…Excuse me, everybody…and there was instant and absolute silence. Oops. Now look what I did.

I handed the mic to Arnold and he did the rest: ludicrous old stories about our travels together had the mob roaring, training advice had young men making mental notes, and his bold encouragement sent pins and needles into us all.

Twenty minutes later, he was ducking his head into the limousine, declaring, "I'll be back" to the delight of his fans.

AN IRON MAN (OR TWO)

Life has become a swift race. I don't want to put on the brakes, but I'm not going to floor it either. Coasting is out. I'll maintain a firm grip on the wheel, watch the curves and let it rip on the straightaway. It's a good ride with good company and I pretend I can pull over anytime I want to. I live in a land of make-believe.

Last week marked the Ironman Pro show, including a three-day fitness expo of 100 vendors, 30 stage events and 120 seminars. The grand affair took place at the Pasadena Center where a recent People's Choice Awards show was staged. (Not a dump.)

You know how special occasions are; you anticipate them, you live them and you re-live them in your memory, and, if all goes well, you don't really know which is the best part. Let me share a few of the highlights of the recent excursion.

Heading out in the rain and darkening skies toward our destination 350 miles south, the traffic thinned, the rain stopped and the daylight vanished about 75 miles down the coast. This is good, because the highway dried off and opened up and the miles went flying by.

Our plan to stop for the night somewhere along the way evaporated with the rain, time and measured distance. By midnight, two wired bombers are looking for a vacancy in a Best Western, the Sheraton full to capacity and us with no reservation due to the change in plans.

We found a room on the other side of the tracks; the door was wide open (strange) and stuffy, the bed was low to the floor and the mattress was less than firm and sloped toward the center. Boiling-hot water bubbled from the bath faucet at a quart a minute, making a gushy sound that wasn't amusing. After I applied my big mitts to the handle and cranked with no success, I wrapped a bath towel around the spout to muffle the noise. Swell.

Good night, sleep tight, don't let the bed bugs bite. Four in the morning, we wake up and our bedroom is now a steam room—mist drifting from the bathroom like early morning fog, water dripping from the ceiling and collecting on the walls forming rivulets and we're soggy.

Welcome to the 24-hour Pasadena Sauna Motel. Sleep and soak. Super swell.

We make it to the Sheraton early, check in and have breakfast. It's Friday. Our skin is still wrinkled, but the ice water is delicious and our spirits are rising as our core temperature drops. Large people are beginning to emerge from elevators, appear around corners and gather in the lobby—a lot of deltoids and dyed skin ready for tomorrow morning's prejudging. Entering a major pro show is no day at the beach, and the bodies look like they could use a sauna and a night's sleep. (Never mind.)

Who's that? Is that Chris Dickerson? Yes, of course.

I haven't seen Chris in 30 years. He stops by our table; we shake hands and shake heads, smiles all around, and promise to catch up later. I spoke to the former Mr. Olympia by phone only a week ago because he appears in Dick Tyler's book, *West Coast Bodybuilding Scene,* and I wanted to send a copy and needed his address. I can give him a copy while he eats breakfast at the Sheraton. Very cool. Chris, an accomplished opera singer, will later present the National Anthem at the Ironman. Looks good, still has his hair.

By eleven, we're hauling boxes of Dick's books and the rest of our gear to the *Iron Man* booth front and center at the Expo in the Civic Center. The place is buzzing as teams complete their displays and early visitors roam the maze of the latest muscle stuff.

Bill and Judy Pearl are there and we're to spend the next three days shoulder to shoulder, meeting and greeting bodybuilding fans, autographing books and posing for photos.

There's much more. Old friends will be gathering and memories will be stirring, new friends will be made and connections established. The internet at work.

The day becomes evening and day one of the expo is a wrap until Saturday morning at 11. We have dinner with Lou Ferrigno and a couple of old friends from the Arnold days. It's been raining all day. Yeah, in fact it rains continually throughout the Iron Man weekend. Wet bodybuilders are everywhere. No complaints, just wet. We refuse to use umbrellas.

We take a long time to order our specialties at an exquisite Chinese restaurant (I have Chinese every 10 to 20 years), agreeing to order five different items from the menu and share them. We're excited, have a lot to talk about, and the food comes in record time.

The plates go around and we dig in, making small mounds of slippery and festively colored meats and vegetables. The chop sticks are pushed aside in favor of forks, and after a flurry of mild comments—delicious, what's this, looks like scallops, tastes like chicken, where's the beef—the table grows quiet but for our chomping and slurping.

We know our Chinese cuisine, this is obvious.

Three minutes into the silence, the waiter returns to tell us we've been served the wrong food—it belongs to that table of six staring at us from the corner. We all agree the food is fine while they're taking it away; I'm eating as fast as I can imagine it—whatever it is—going into the dumpster in the alley. I actually stick the young waitress in the hand with my fork as she reaches for my plate.

Our actual meal comes soon enough, and the whole plate-sharing process begins once again. We're practiced, less desperately hungry, and a bit embarrassed for not noticing the difference between Chicken Gun Pow and Scallops Cow Moo.

Good night, you guys. Next time we'll order steak and potatoes. See you at the Expo.

And the rains came down.

Might I interpose a bit of muscle-building information? The Hulk eats the same foods with the same methodology as the Bomber.

Obviously.

It's not late and we go to our room with a longing for quiet privacy and a flat, firm bed; tomorrow we pick up Dick Tyler at the Burbank airport, 9:00 sharp. Dick is 10 years older than I and is the author of *West Coast Bodybuilding Scene.* He's been a dedicated Doctor of Chiropractic for 45 years and has been out of the bodybuilding scene, which he once wrote about prolifically, lovingly. He trains himself, and heals others. He doesn't know Ronnie Coleman from Ronald McDonald, and hasn't been to a major bodybuilding show where bodybuilders achieve the proportions of tractors and trailers and trucks.

He will flip.

He'll also help introduce our recent publication to the Iron Man spectators and visitors as soon as he resumes his composure.

By mid-afternoon, fans are taking pictures of Don Howorth, Bill Pearl, Chris Dickerson, Lou Ferrigno, Dick and me as we line up arms over shoulders, or clustered together, grinning and yakking. Gene Mozee and his famous camera are clicking away and Laree, having fun watching this motley collection, finally manages to sneak around taking her joyful candids.

There's Cory Everson, whose beauty increases with time. We share a big hug and fond exchange; she's the greatest. Yo, Richie—Rich

Gaspari, handsome and strong, is researching and preparing his own line of products. We're both from Jersey; hence, we're old buds.

Bill "Kaz" Kazmier, particularly good at lifting things, is lifting everyone's spirits as he visits friends between scheduled power demonstrations. Scot Mendelson and his power team are a good group—did I mention large and strong and large?—and give me two thumbs up for the Top Squat. Or else!

So many people, so many exchanges, so much encouragement. Samir Bannout, looking very strong, grabs me from a roving crowd at the press conference to introduce me to his training partner, a building.

Whenever I get anxious or feel crowded I mutter, "Aren't you glad you're not competing?"

Whatever is going on at the pre-judging, backstage and in the hotel rooms of the competitors has got to be more frantic than missing that second meal or losing the car in the parking lot or going the wrong way on one-way Pasadena Ave—worse than a midnight sauna on a soggy, sagging mattress that will swallow you up. I love the rain.

Time for the night show. Leroy Colbert and I sit together at the Saturday night main event. We, too, are former Weider employees (more accurately, physique stars), and have a record that goes back to 1956. Neither of us has aged, of course, and we talk enthusiastically above the clamor of the packed house.

The brave and bikini-clad gals march onstage, and Armand Tanny to my right groans his approval.

They march offstage, they're on, they're off and on again. They stand, turn, flex and smile; flex, turn, stand, smile and are off. One more time, girls, please, thank you. Someone—oops—forgot to judge the ladies at the mid-day prejudging. Some are beauties, some are cuties, some are big and mean and they're all tough.

The judges work hard—late, but hard—and make their choices.

The Iron Man contenders total 15 and I'm exposed to the most recent trend in posing and presentation. Looks the same to me. They are thick and mighty, and again the judges complete their task.

While Dexter Jackson receives his award as number one Iron Man and greets the spectators from the MC's mic—an apology for not looking as good as he will at the Arnold in two weeks—the satisfied yet uninterested crowd sluggishly makes its way toward the exit doors.

"Move along, folks, you can't stand in the aisles. Move along, we're trying to clean and close. Move along," says the security guard for the Pasadena Civic Auditorium.

I want to yell, "We love ya, Dexter, really."

"Move along, folks."

"Yeah, yeah."

The rain is wet, and cold.

John Balik is the man behind *Iron Man Magazine* and the promoter of the Iron Man Pro Show. We've been friends since Joe Gold opened his gym doors to us. He's calm, cool and collected through the whole project; his team loves him, and he's been hard at it since he bought Ironman from Perry and Mabel Rader in 1986.

We're honored to be among the invited guests. In the years to come, he hopes to bring the champs from earlier days together for fun and memories and health for the soul.

An experiment in longevity and quality of life.

A BLAST OF BUCKSHOT

Where does one begin when talking about the Arnold Classic Expo? The whole affair grows from year to year, with its ever-expanding fitness mobs and ever-expanding competitors—several breaking the 300-pound barrier.

The Expo alone features professional record-setting powerlifting and strongman championships, major martial arts and gymnastic competitions, arm wrestling contests and world-class women's bodybuilding and fitness awards. Demonstrations, comedians and artistic acts of strength and balance fill the front and center stages and giant screen as a variety of competitors rotate positions.

Of course, this is a back-up to, or backed up by, the vendors—all 600 of them. They dig into tight trenches to greet and meet the enthusiastic visitors, displaying wares that include endless concoctions to build huge muscles and eliminate masses of fat (so, vat else is new?); provide instant tans and remove unwanted hair forever; transform mediocre gym sales to sky-rocketing gym sales and, if you keep your eyes open, there are those who'll make you the person you always wanted to be, have the potential to be, are destined to be, or who you really are. Others insure you, dress you, photograph you, enlist you—Army, Navy, Air Force and Marines—or customize your muscle car or power Harley.

Never a dull moment. Look, there's Sergio. Holy Cow!

Hey, there's Louie, the Hulk.

No way. There's Pearl. Unreal!

Omigosh, that's Bill Grant and Lee Labrada and Danny Padilla.

Pinch me!

Gaspari?! Wha?

Is that Zane? Insane!

Gasp! Cory. Gasp!

No, yes, erp. Not Tommy Kono and Isaac Berger?! Ike!

Yo. It's Westside's Louie Simmons. Geez, Louise!

Get a grip. That's steel-hands John Brookfield. Yikes spikes!

Ho hum. There's Dave Draper.

Who? Dan Dapner. Who? Dern Dipler. Who? You know, the blonde bopper. The what? Never mind.

I was holding down a corner of the Torque Exhibit, a four-booth display of equipment and manufacturing skills. Scott Sonnon and his vigorous martial arts team demonstrated their unique Clubbell training methods, and I periodically squatted to the tune of the Top Squat in A-major.

Scot Mendelson's teammate, Larry Pollack, picked up a Top Squat for himself and his weightlifting buds, and James Mendoza, Ed Corney's training partner, grabbed one to erase their squatting limitations. Then Will, a Louie Simmons recordholder, dragged away one of the units for some mean team handling. More were sold to other avid lifters until there were no more.

Huge bodies and a lot of flesh were on display at the multitude of rockin' booths, sufficient supplies of deltoids, biceps and triceps roved this year's double-wide aisles. You didn't have to wait all day to catch a glimpse of the latest in female cleavage, so I'm told. Yet overall, the crowd was nicer, calmer, less rowdy and, perhaps, more graceful…unless you were handing out free t-shirts. Toss anything free into the crowd and they instantly change…Jekyll and Hyde…voraciously hungry hawk chicks…spawning salmon…a surviving, near-distinct species. Trophy hunters.

Do not get in the way if you favor your life or limb. It's all in good fun and reveals a healthy zeal awaiting its timely direction to the iron and steel.

I don't know about the people waiting in lines a hundred yards long to get a free cheapo plastic bottle in which to mix their protein. These might be the same folks who sit on the leg extension between sets and read a magazine or fiddle with their cell phones while leaning against a squat rack. Hello. Get a clue.

Protein powder can be eaten by the spoonful followed by a gulp of water. Boom-Zoom.

Arnold passed by at one point on his way to the Expo stage to greet everyone and announce his editorship of *Muscle and Fitness* and *Flex* magazines. His focus was straight forward, his smile fixed in place, his pace quick with the California Highway Patrol on his heels. Where does this guy get his energy, determination, motivation and courage? Arnold gets up every morning, splashes water on his face, walks over to the cliff and jumps.

Skirting a frenzied mound of savages shredding what looked like a bloodied free tanktop, I headed for the Brookfield Man of Strength. I'm a John Brookfield admirer. His hand strength is phenomenal and is only surpassed by his Godly wisdom. He and his wife and 10-year-old daughter were just unwrapping their lunch when we arrived...barged in like over-excited goofs is more like it.

Eating and going to the john are the two most difficult challenges exhibitors face during the long Arnold expo. Bending a 3/4-inch rod into a tight coil or squatting six plates is a medium task by comparison.

The five of us mixed like good spices and found we had a lot in common. We shared stories while their dear daughter lifted a 50-pound kettlebell repeatedly for the fun of it.

Before leaving, John offered one of his metal figures composed of spikes bent by his mighty hands and uniquely welded together. There was a chromed length of thick steel twisted into concentric circles and 10- and 20-penny nails bent and joined to resemble iron and steel characters lifting weights. Today we have on our mantle John's 10- and 20-penny spikes distorted by muscle and might in the posture of man in prayer.

There are notables everywhere and the excitement and energy spills into the corridors and walkways of the exhibition hall, into the hotel lounges and surrounding restaurants. The mingling and networking goes on through the night for days on end. Making plans is important and necessary, but just as important is to throw your time in the air and let it come down as it will.

Jeff O'Connell, a longtime friend and east coast senior writer for *Muscle and Fitness*, organized a Harry Benson photo shoot of bodybuilders from the golden years. A stately Englishman some years older than me, Harry achieved worldwide notoriety for his photography of famous political leaders and activists, sport stars and entertainers. His grand works include such luminaries as Winston Churchill, Princess Diana, the Beatles, JFK, Ford, Clinton, Ali and my buddy, Johnny Carson.

Naturally, I was chosen to be one of them. I know, I know. Sometimes life's a big circus and the clowns get loose.

About mid-afternoon on Saturday, the day of the Classic, Jeff joins me at a book-signing to escort us to a nearby conference room, where we find Harry and his assistant ready for action.

Now, it wouldn't be so bad if I hadn't just had laser surgery to remove some mild and innocuous marks on my cheeks and forehead (strictly cosmetic and ego-driven). One day in the middle of the winter one has this done, 10 days go by, and who cares or remembers. That dumb blotching goes away and it's cool.

Not exactly. The dumb blotching was replaced by a face full of black and blue dots the size of BBs. It looks like a blast of buckshot. Harry looks at me and blinks.

He looks at Jeff, and his jaw quivers. Disappointed.

He looks around the room and uncharacteristically scratches his head. Discouraged.

He looks at his assistant, who's looking out the door. Dismal.

He regroups with dignity and we sit at a table full of Cheezits and unfinished cokes from an earlier news conference.

"Tell you what," he says in proper British, "sit with your hands under your chin like this."

He demonstrates the ordinary, relaxed position, and smiles.

I worked tris the day I left town—real hard…in advance of the forced layoff to follow—and carrying luggage and gear through miles of airports didn't help my elbows one bit either. I try his pose, but succeed only in straining my chin forward to barely touch my extended knuckles. I'm about to tear up from the effort, and admit I can't do it and tell him why. This he doesn't "get," but at least I know you do.

"How about this," he says as if addressing the keeper of a creature losing its fur in clumps, "lay your hands flat on the table before you."

His camera is at the ready should I accidentally assume a handsome, manly or attractive pose or position. By now, I'm laughing in little private fits.

I lob my meat hooks onto the table and a coke splashes almost without notice.

My hands have a few marks—scabs from minor wounds gained by aggressive lifting—and he returns the camera with the big lens to the table.

Harry's looking whooped.

After 15 minutes of squirming and clicking infrequently, we discover the photo shoot has become a private seminar on health, fitness and the bodybuilding field, about which Harry knew nothing.

His calm manner and harmless questions to put me at ease and cause camera-useful responses—I'm hip—provoked in-depth answers and critical comments more engaging than the tiresome act of snapshot collecting.

He's learning, he learned. We made silk from discarded wool.

I'm still unsure of the purpose of the photo session.

Fifty IronOnliners gathered for dinner on Friday night at a crazy subterranean Italian restaurant to share lasagna, veal and chicken and fine conversation for three hours. Parcels of friends bumped into each other at various eateries for breakfast, lunch or late-night snacks. Friends from Florida, a *Flex* editor from LA, and a strength coach from a southern university sit around peacefully at the day's end in oversized chairs.

We talk above the din of the hotel's opening and closing elevator doors and the less-than-hurried footfalls of the evening's thinning traffic. We're a tired bunch; standing, hurrying, carrying, standing, smiling, talking, posing and smiling takes the wind from beneath your wings, bombardiers. The hotel room becomes a refuge.

Funny thing I never get used to: time goes by, there's no stopping it and there's no slowing it down. Neither can I make it go faster.

LOCKED IN A TIME ZONE WITHOUT A CLUE

Browsing my email this past week, I came across a message listing the top-10 Mr. Olympia competitors according to placement. My first reaction was, "What the? Mr. Olympia!! So soon, or is it late this year? Hmm..."

Then it occurred to me how little I know about the muscle scene. I'm in awe of Ronnie Coleman and Jay Cutler and Gunter Schlierkamp; they are altogether fantastic, magnificent and overwhelming...dare I exclude breathtaking and bewildering from my adjectival commentary.

However, the remaining seven contenders were unknown to me. They could have been roto rooters, insurance salesman or card sharks for all I knew—I had no clue. These men stood above the rest in the musclebuilding world. They toiled under the iron in the gym and battled fiercely for position on the field of competition. They're victors onstage and heroes before crowds. They are stars in the theater I once played, crowned royalty in the courts I once reigned.

I paused for a second and mused. Have I become one of those peculiar people unable or unwilling to face present-day life with all its changes, complexities and distress? Am I locked in the Golden Era time zone, safe and glorifying?

Am I a relic in a museum of time gone by, an item of curiosity from long ago—a tarnished, slightly warped drying thing that still works if one was careful in its handling? You can touch it, but don't drop it. Look at that, will ya? Its head bobbles to this day.

Am I out of touch, old-fashioned and behind the times? Is what I know, the information and understanding I've gained over the years, of any worth, or is it, like the phonograph, obsolete? And the tune I sing, is it the same old tune sung those many years ago? Off-key, scratchy?

I knew the answers, and there were three: Yeah, right! Gimme a break! Get outta town. I don't think so! Not exactly!! What kind of stupid question is that?

That's six, I lied.

I'd be going backwards and losing ground if I stepped into the bodybuilding world of today. The guys are the greatest, but the path of travel, the environment and the players are as real as Rolexes hustled on the internet.

I thank God I'm not a contender today or I'd be standing at a precarious crossroads, heads it's left, tails it's right. Rolex knockoff or sundial.

The truth is, I don't care for bodybuilding anymore than I care for the WWF, Monster Truck derbies or roulette. Same with sports; I lost interest in football and basketball after I graduated high school and no longer played the games. Rooting on Monday nights or sunny Sundays afternoons just doesn't happen for me.

Someone told me that such behavior is a symptom of an antisocial oddball. Who me? I live in a cabin in the woods and wear a shoebox over my head when I go to the market at three in the morning for groceries. Say hello and I twitch.

That's just focused. I'm focused. And dedicated. Focused and dedicated, that's me.

Ronnie has a book on the market, *Hardcore*, outlining his training methods. What could he possibly tell us to help us achieve the physique he has? What terms does he use, what language does he speak? Are his weights made of tungsten; does he train in special gravity-control rooms?

When building his biceps, does he simply perform curls as described by other trainers or does he use cryptic codes and formulas to express the complexity of the arm exercise and the intensity applied?

Shoulder width: Is this accomplished with presses and lateral raises as we know them, or are there new dimensions of exercise our ordinary finite bodies and minds cannot conceive? Increase ohms by seven with each successive repetition until a warning light flashes.

And how about food? What is it about protein we don't know, and those energy-supplying carbs and fats? Does one eat every 90 minutes and sleep between meals? Eat the limbs of oak trees and gnaw on granite? What is it, what don't we know?

Pictures of Ron, eight-time Mr. Olympia, are indescribable and, for some of us, inspiring. But, looking at the man for inspiration to build one's muscles is not unlike studying a battleship gliding through the Pacific to learn how to swim.

But as for me, give me a protein powder and two hours at the gym and I'll figure something out on my own. It'll be the secret of the day, though I still say there are no secrets.

Today is a good example: Walking from my vehicle toward the gym was like walking the plank. Monday and Tuesday were upper body days and I pushed vigorously. I set no records, received no medals of honor and I drew no blood. Fine!

But recently, leg days have presented a problem. "Ugh" is the three-letter word I use to express my attitude toward, my performance during, and the residual effect after the workout.

Gasping has replaced deep breathing, and heavy weights have given way to (gasp! see what I mean?) moderate weights. The whole catastrophe puts me in an ugh mood. This is not fun, smart, wise, healthy or good.

It's bad.

To obviate the ughnicity of the training session and hopefully overcome the decline in leg performance, I resorted to leg presses trisetted with thigh curls and calves. I then proceeded to the squat rack for full squats. I finished with rope tucks and hanging leg raises until I dropped…I dropped fast and hard.

The secret of the day was submitting to a decline in leg strength and endurance and daring—daring to push myself into a dreaded, hateful overworked zone. The big muscles place a major demand on the heart and lungs and vascular system, and I'm fed up and I'm not going to take it anymore.

The last month of leg workouts have had me in a tizzy; I refused to let go and the thought of leg days made me miserable. Despite my heroics (stupidity), the leg sessions diminished in every way. I was lost and alone.

The second secret of the day was lowering the reps. The higher reps, though not high at all, were doing me in. Each rep over six had my heart thumping like a wombat and my lungs sucking oxygen from the next county. The modifications were minor, obvious and humbling, and reduced the chance of injury and increased the certainty of continued leg training, squats included.

I felt blasted, but not wounded or destroyed. I limped, but did not crawl. I smiled. These are good signs.

My day beneath the loaded bar will come again.

You can teach some of the dogs all the tricks, and all the dogs some of the tricks, but some dogs you can't teach nothin.'

This experience is simple and everyday, yet regularly causes overdoses and wrist-slashings. I hope by sharing it, we might both grow stronger and live longer. Maybe time is catching up, or maybe I need to grow up.

I'm praying it's neither.

In fact, it may very well be that I'm acting too much like an older person—worrying, doubting, wheezing—and it's just a minor anomaly in enzyme activity. So obvious...

I like flying at night with my lights out.

BOMBS AWAY

There's an impressive list of ever-growing personal appearances I'm to make, from San Diego to Pittsburgh, with a quick stop in London for charm.

Then there's the upcoming *E! True Hollywood Story*—lights, camera and action. Wowee! But let me tell you a favorite story, a recent one that more clearly portrays the bomber I know.

Hayward is 50 miles northeast of Santa Cruz and is the home of Protein Research Lab, the manufacturer of the Bomber Blend protein. I make a trip to the lab every month or so to pick up a supply of the precious powder. I dare not run out and risk muscular denial, depression and scurvy. My last run was in mid-January, early one Thursday afternoon—sweet timing to beat the mean Bay Area commute traffic.

Rocko, the warehouse super, loaded my pickup with two shrink-wrapped pallets and declared me ready to go. I stood back, studied the towering stack of boxed tubs and scratched my head. Looks goofy, but it's not overweight. Okay, Santa Cruz or bust.

I hop in, rev the engine and I'm outta there before the working mobs cut loose. Traffic is my enemy.

The power and the stability of my Toyota gives me confidence and I move from the friendly, boring slow lane of 880 to the alluring yet frenzied fast lane. No one 200 yards in front of or behind me and I'm sailing. Both hands on the wheel, synchronized eyes on the road and side-view mirrors and I'm flying. No highway patrol in sight, I level off at 70. Risk is my secret companion.

That plastic wrap is making a tremendous racket as it flaps to the rhythm of the wind.

Three miles down 880, the tempo of the shrink-wrap clatter perceptibly changes and causes me to wonder. I tilt my electric side-view mirror upward to inspect my cargo and watch, as if in slow motion, four cases of that remarkable Bomber Blend, one followed by another, and another, tumble out the back of my sturdy four-wheel drive truck.

This is not funny and I'm not laughing.

Gotta get outta the dumb fast lane fast and onto a clear shoulder. Negotiating, maneuvering, shifting, braking…and I'm stopped roadside and stepping out of the truck. This doesn't look good.

A small compact speeds by, the guy blowing his horn, yelling and waving his fists.

I'm topside, securing the reduced load and craning to see the road behind me. Thoughts crowd my head, like what a loss, cops are gonna come, get the truck off the freeway: all those embarrassing, selfish thoughts that expose who you really are.

I hop off the truck and run up a rise, hoping to get a better look at the crime scene. All I can see is a white billowing cloud the size of a Costco, with powdery cars and trucks bursting out of the near side like baffled pigeons of a mischievous highway joke.

I'm in awe.

The puffy pigeons keep coming, and I turn and run for my conspicuous metallic-red over-stacked Japanese four-wheeler.

It's a short dash across a narrow 100-foot weedy shoulder strewn with a roadways' collection of debris. I'm making good time as I study the passing traffic, hoping they don't pull over and flog me.

Suddenly, I'm down and rolling in the dirt.

I get up, and down I go again.

My legs are tangled in a rusty wire hoop that came out of nowhere and as I lie on the ground, kicking and crawling and angrily tugging at the tricky device, I visualize my plight.

The already distressed passers-by see this oversized, red-faced buffoon in comedic tragedy, flailing and bewildered, staggering and stumbling as if possessed.

Somewhere inside, I laugh as I hurry to return to the highway and retrace my ignominious steps.

Was there a tragedy, an accident of consequence, a car out of control, or has everyone escaped with little more than a healthy fright from the exploding vanilla powder and momentary loss of reality? Ten minutes later I'm in the slow lane, exploring the target zone and see only wisps of drifting whey and calcium caseinate. Fifty pounds of branch-chain amino acids and anti-oxidants drift in swirls at the highway's edge, not a tub or cardboard box as evidence.

I resume my slow lane voyage to my homeland and recall with a spontaneous burst of repressed laughter the tubs of vanilla as they, in locked-time, retreat from my tailgate in the general direction of the blacktop and the oncoming innocent players.

Still today, I await a knock on my door by a uniformed policeman, a lawyer and or angry mob looking for justice in regard to the 880 Random Blizzard Bombing. My life has taken many turns; the bizarre episodes are unending. Next week: *The Day I Did Squats with Aliens from Outer Space: Episode One.*

It's a grand day, and I'm off to the gym to steal a pump.

THE SUN SETS OVER MISSOURI

I felt like a stray dog at a horse show—the US Bench Press Nationals were held in St. Louis this past weekend and I was there displaying the Top Squat. Nearly 200 lifters, men and women from all over, were there with their friends and families, geared up to set some records and have a ton of heavyweight fun. They're a hearty, robust group.

Rickey Dale Crain, a powerlifting champion from the golden days (powerlifting and bodybuilding Golden Eras coincide, coincidentally), was front and center with his high-energy support and colorful arrangement of lifting gear and materials.

Get this: He entered his first powerlifting meet the same spring I entered my first physique contest (Mr. N.J.) in 1963. Neither of us have put down the weights down. Weird is good!

The larger-than-average spectators sat in fold-up chairs and came and went as they pleased (who's gonna stop them?), as the competitors warmed up in an intense backstage area. Strict procedures were followed by each lifter before approaching the bench on the platform; strict judging was in place. The honor and professionalism in presentation was admirable.

Where's a camera when you need one? One dude with a shaved was seated on two folding chairs. His outstretched arms busted through a t-shirt minus its sleeves, and encompassed the two seats at his sides, where two other skinhead dudes of near-equal bulk—one-chair per occupant with no room to wiggle—sat casually as only 375-pounders can. Their necks looked like the columns used to support an interstate overpass, and their shoulders, traps and arms mounded together, the foothills of the Sierras.

Sun was coming through an open doorway to the west and their taut skin glistened. They drank little cans of beer and didn't move for hours. Saving their energy for Sunday, the day the big boys let 'er loose.

Lots of meaty broad shoulders moved around, as records were attempted and records were set. I milled around with the Torque travel crew, demonstrated our impressive tools and added up the experiences. Of course, big people love thick handles and the Top Squat to accommodate their tough training and add protection and ability to their movements.

As the first day wound down, a small entourage of Mobile Christian Strongmen appeared in the parking lot to cause commotion, demonstrate feats of strength, hold an impromptu strongman contest and praise the Lord. Some off-the-wall entertainment was a welcome lift to the routine lifts we studied for more than eight hours with ever-glazing eyes. Paul Smith, a 32-year-old, 330-pound, 6'6," Kentucky-strong, strongman grinned like a gorilla in love.

As the sun set over Missouri (yes, the sun also sets over Missouri), we moved out to the parking lot and grabbed folding chairs, a car bumper, piece of grass or stone curb to watch the events unfold.

And it was exactly what we hoped it would be: a boisterous engagement of spiritually energized speakers, mismatched music, crazy stories from powerful real-time strongmen and powerlifters, huge balls of solid concrete being lifted to the shoulder, obscure and awesome tractor parts deadlifted or carried for distance and speed, chains being snapped, bars of steel twisted into coils and sledge hammers breaking cinder blocks on some enthusiastic youth delicately supported on a bed of nails.

I'm next…me, me!

My favorite carnival act was performed by the lovable and persuasive Paul Smith. He bent 10-penny nails in his hands and tossed them to the kids in the crowd for a warm-up. He then moved to the wrecking ball, a common tool found at any ordinary demolition site. Solid steel and the size of a basketball, the 100-pound black beauty was rigged with a stout eyehook for industrial applications.

Paul bends over, sticks his middle finger in the eyehook, cleans the hunk to his shoulder and presses and lowers it gently. Thud. Before the day was over, he bent a pound of nails and heaved the wrecking ball 11 times. His finger no longer fit into the eyehook…it was strangely swollen. Paul says the swelling will be gone in two weeks and the finger will be stronger, the silver lining to every black-and-blue cloud.

On Sunday, we were treated to bench pressing attempts and successful completions in the 500–700-pound range. Plates were flying like pancakes and the spotters, like short-order cooks, were working overtime.

I must remind you I'm a mono-minded musclebuilder who loves weight training and has incorporated heavy lifting throughout his lifting efforts. I know the feel and the need, but know nothing of the powerlifting as a sport. I'm impressed with what I see, like the gal who got three white lights for her 400-plus bench, an 80-year-old guy full of vigor and heart easily push 237 (not his best), and some big fella set a world drug-free record of 711. (I missed the names because I'm a major schlump.

The last powerlifting meet I attended was nearly 30 years ago, in an abandoned storefront with newspaper covering the windows, wooden benches for the spectators, yelling instead of a mic, air leaking in from the backdoor and stirring up chalk and dust, moms with squealing kids and a splintery plywood platform for the competition. Anybody could enter; all you needed was 20 bucks.

It seems there are now more than four lifting associations with different rules and regulations; some are open and anything goes, some restrict drug use, and others don't allow lifting shirts or drugs. The latter seems to be the most authentic test of strength, the former the most…um…impressive—and somewhere in between the most popular. It's much like bodybuilding today with its various facets, dimensions and levels of acceptance. Confused me, but maybe you have this down pat.

Before I came home, I spent a lot of time touring the dead ends and hidden streets of St. Louis with my good IronOnline bud, Tom Canavan and his family. Former gym owners, present-day bombers and lovers of life, we watched the days unfold with curious amazement.

It's fun being oddballs in oddball settings. You don't feel strange or out of place in an ordinary world; you realize how strange and out of place the ordinary world is. Round and soft and undermuscled—eating and sleeping and unaware—video games and cell phones at the ready.

I periodically ate tuna from a can and drank water from a discarded diet Pepsi container in the packed room of the Holiday Inn where the contest was held. I was wallowing in my peculiar behavior where peculiarity had no bounds. It's the little things of life that make a big difference. Odd is in. In is out.

This is odd for a bomber: The flights knocked me out.

SMASH BASH

The last-ever Santa Cruz Bomber Bash came and went with the roar and power of a speeding freight train. There were whispers of people arriving from different parts of the planet as early as Wednesday, sightings on Thursday and by mid-morning Friday, they formed at the World Gym into an eager and boisterous crowd.

Cheering spectators for the chinning challenge spilled out the back door as the grinning, determined contestants circled the bar positioned high above bobbing heads. Adrenalin, encouragement, enthusiasm and applause raised the strong and bold to the occasion, each exhibiting more reps than ever before.

Pull, pull, pull…one more rep…you've got it, you've got it!!!

The winning number was 28—the quantity of repetitions was not the point. The point was the laughter, smiling faces, physical exertion, mutual support and oneness of mind. Here we were, devoted IronOnline forum members, most of whom had never before met in person, hanging onto each other and chattering like long-lost family.

What do we know that everyone else seems to have missed? What is it in the iron that causes such magnetism?

A mile away as a crow doth fly, there's a commercial kitchen full of volunteers attending the food preparations: homemade salads, Texas beans and side dishes. This is a noisy and comical scene with giant pots, huge bowls and heaps of vegetables on every available countertop undergoing a chaotic order of boiling, filling, slicing and dicing. Periodically, someone leaves his post and a camera silently emerges at the right moment to record the mess and the messy. Smile…oops! Too late! Hehe!

The gathering at the gym grew larger through the early afternoon before it broke into junks and hunks, bits and pieces toward evening. At 7:30, we reformed into one vital mass for simple and scrumptious chow, more excited conversation, and—for anyone who could keep his or her sleepy eyes open (gettin' late, kids), a showing of *Don't Make Waves.*

When the movie ended, the remaining 50 bombers of the original 125 stumbled upstairs and off to bed like drowsy kids at a slumber party. Good night, sleep tight, don't let the bed bugs bite.

By 8 o'clock Saturday morning, the Martin Crew is organizing the barbecue, no cute backyard grill for Mom, Pop and the kids and Auntie Sue and Uncle Lou…please, can I have another hotdog. The grill at the manicured edge of a redwood forest is 10x4 feet, and the serving table is longer than one of those preposterous stretch limos you see following itself down the freeway. Food's collecting everywhere and they're loving the culinary effort.

Three-hundred yards away from the smoldering charcoal, the gym is humming with its usual weekend warriors and the small invasion of conquering heroes from across the land and sea.

Bill Pearl and his small entourage of friends and family have already trained, opening the doors at 5:45 to beat the gravity and heat and make as much noise as they want and need. He promises to be back at 11:00 to tell everyone what he does, why, when and how. I'll be completely awake, scrubbed and de-grouched by then, and intend to stand by his side and be of service in any way I can. Another bottle of water, Bill? A mint?

The World Gym is one of those neat, well-planned neighborhood gyms—just the right size, simple colors, high ceilings, lots of air and light, sufficient sound, great equipment, tons of weight and no silliness. It's the kind of gym you fall in love with, the kind that's becoming rare on the emerging horizons, an endangered species, a white rhino, a spotted leopard. (Save a real gym in your neighborhood today. Make donations: used Rolexes, diamond pendants, gold bracelets, pearl necklaces, rare coins or dear Grandmother's broach.)

The sky is blue and the sun is warm and the gym floor is looking like the morning rush at Grand Central Station. The mic squeals as the sound is adjusted and 200 animated bodies become still and their voices silent.

Someone say something, I beg under my breath, each second sounding like a minute. Oh, boy! That someone would be me, wouldn't it? I fiddle with a cable and a switch, and my suave yet commanding voice is blasted loud and clear to the next county like a low-rider's blaring boom-box.

Everyone ducks and grimaces; we're off to a good start.

After my brief introduction where I dazzle the brilliant assemblage of ironminds with my charm, wit and good humor, Bill and I begin our question-and-answer seminar. Bill insists upon going first, but I quickly point out that the whole thing was my idea. He then declares, childishly I thought, that he's the guest of honor and it's his choice, not mine. I say, "Bull," and lunge for his mic, when Laree comes stomping from the crowd, video camera in hand and scowling, and tells me I'm being a jerk. I hate that.

By this time Ed Corney, the brute, emerges from nowhere and masterfully engages me in a step-over-toe-hold, to which I submit immediately. Worse yet, I had to apologize to Bill before the gang and he then answered the first question of the planned QnA. Drat!

Talks are so formal, stiff and teacher-like. They tend to hide the personality of the speaker behind a poorly prepared presentation, and compel the audience to listen to whatever subject the speaker chooses. "Today, let's discuss fast-twitch muscles and how they compare to slow-twitch muscles by calibrating the internal forces applied consecutively, separately and in alternate sequences throughout a series of rapid and non-rapid resistance movements. Did you bring your notepad and pen? Good! Now, then, students, as clearly indicated on this chart..."

Just say no.

I loved every minute of the two-and-a-half-hour exchange between Bill Pearl, the eager crowd and me: pure entertainment, unvarnished truth and a pleasant peak into the lives of everyone who cared or dared to speak.

The level of information discussed was not profound and no one walked away highly enlightened. What was gained was affirmation of the things we already know, often forget and sometimes doubt. There's nothing new under the musclebuilder's sun or the bodybuilder's posing lights—no secrets, no worthy apparatus and no high-tech breakthroughs. There's just us—you and me—and hard work, the basics and common sense...as if the truth wasn't enough.

By early afternoon, everyone migrates to the grassy park across the isolated street. Smoke rises steadily and deliciously from the fiery charcoal pit, as tritip, chicken and salmon grill to perfection. We're old friends with healthy appetites and hearts full of banter and affection. No one's alone, shyness has receded, conversations have developed and we send for more meat (good call) before the sun gets anywhere near casting shadows.

People are eating Marianne's ice cream between servings of meat and salads and garlic bread. Why not?

Especially insightful, I heard someone remark, "I've never seen 200 people gathered together laughing and having this much fun without considerable alcohol to drink."

The day was long, packed and, as expected, eventually came to a slow end. The group with plans ready for the evening dispersed; the leftovers and utensils, bowls and pots were stashed in our homebound vehicles, and the area was swept clean. How empty, how quiet…the embers still aglow.

"Thanks everybody, see ya tomorrow…yeah, at the gym in the morning."

It's only 7:30 and I'm thinking of crashing…a mellow crash…after we empty the assorted gear and rinse the pots and bowls.

Sunday is a planned brunch at the hotel, goodbye to the travelers from Florida and Texas, Michigan and Minnesota, Jersey and New York, Pennsylvania and Louisiana, LA and Sacramento and San Francisco. You get the picture.

A large handful of bombers remained in town, extending their vacations with plans of visiting San Francisco to the north and Big Sur and Monterey to the south. Thus, they were among those of us who met at the marina in the early afternoon for an off-shore cruise on a 50-foot sailing yacht.

It is slightly amazing to sail off the coast of Santa Cruz on the Pacific Ocean for a few hours in the warm sun and pure air. Forty beautiful people sat back or wandered carefully around the windblown deck—duck when the captain rings the bell, or the swinging boom will take you for a precarious and embarrassing ride.

More chatter, more delight. You had to be there.

It was at the yacht harbor that most of the last goodbyes were said, none of which were easy.

Words cannot describe...

LONDON TOWN

This not a late report on how to get huge and ripped, but skipping a weekly writing deadline is not unlike skipping a workout. You've gotta get one in there, no matter how brief, to keep the pace, the continuity, the pump and the blood moving. We got in from London late last night and are shaking the twitches of travel from our bones and our brains. The necessary phone calls have been made to reconstruct some falling bridges and snuff a small outbreak of brush fires and we are ready for the iron and steel.

London to us as tourists was a magical experience, like the lady sawed in two while stuffed in a decorative box. The music played dramatically as the magician applied his trade without effort or emotion. He pierced his lovely model with swords and separated the bisected halves as she smiled. You watch in familiar suspense, already knowing the outcome. The trick done, m'lady hops out of her enclosure to twirl and spin from the fingertips of mysterious man in black. Bows, applause, astonishment and end of act. England is grand and lovely.

For two Americans on the loose from Santa Cruz, London was a seven-day adventure. Day one, we sat aboard the aircraft of Flight 284 at San Francisco International for five hours before being requested to disembark due to mechanical failure. The journey was to resume the next day in the early afternoon. Fine.

The 747 jumbo jet had been full. Travelers resembling zombies were transported in a preposterous convoy to a new Residence Inn, where, after being carelessly lost in the vast outskirts of SF, we were fed warm pizza as a late dinner. I didn't have the nerve or energy to rebel—protein powder and tuna judiciously stashed in my carryon case to the rescue.

We slept (sort of) to the distant rumble of arriving and departing aircraft.

The flight eventually departed and arrived at Heathrow Airport early the (next) following afternoon. The behavior and mood of the crew and passenger ensemble were remarkable. This others and I accredited to the fact that they were mostly English. Americans, I suspect, would have caused a riot.

Dragging around far too much luggage, we staggered to the bus ramps, where we waited for our connection to the hotel in Winslow and the Oscar Heidenstam Awards later that evening.

Hitting the sidewalk, we immediately noted that it was very cold and rainy and gloomy. We shivered and waited and waited and shivered. Everyone drove on the wrong side of the street and the wrong side of the car in the wildest synchronicity. We shivered.

The Oscar Heidenstam Awards Dinner is another story for another time, grand simplicity in love of the sport of iron and steel. I was honored and fussed over and made true friends. The refined English pride was presented to us in big-hearted portions.

The one-day affair ended with breakfast the following brisk morning. The plate was quite full of gammon (ham), bangers (sausage) and country eggs, and we passed on the appetizing mounds of black pudding, which we later learned was generous amounts of animal blood mixed with a grainy meal. May we be excused from the table, please? Gotta pack.

Layers of clothes limited the cold to our ears and sniffling noses, and we aimed for London and our next hotel via busses, the Tube and on foot, avoiding taxis, as they are, we were told, expensive and suspicious. Somewhere in the midst of our hasty travels, Laree let out a yelp and thumped her forehead with the meaty palm of her hand. Have mercy, something's wrong: Our passports and airline tickets were still in the blue bag left on one of those crazy busses.

We sent out a plea through one of the drivers, and after a stretched out 40 minutes, a company car appeared at the roadside bearing our documents. Profuse thanks and we were back in action, never to forget the honesty and kindness that warmed our shivering hearts.

Once settled, our old and classy British hotel served us well, where we were anywhere in the heart of London, where the city people settle into apartments, eat, live and sleep. They scurry around high speed all day and into the night, from shop to shop, from the underground to the bus to the car to the motorbike. Starbuck's line every street, as do McDonald's, Burger Kings and fish n' chip pubs. Stand on any corner and you'll hear French, German, multi-Asian languages, Pakistani, Russian, Spanish and other sounds of communication. The cacophony is symphonic and tireless.

We visited where we were able in the three remaining days, hungry to observe and absorb something more than England from the tiresome tongue of a tour guide. We took to the Tube and stopped at the various familiar districts whose names we recognized from Beatle songs, movies and *CNN:* Piccadilly Circus, Trafalgar Square, Buckingham, Parliament, and The Thames.

Big Ben bonged for us at 3:15, but I was too cold to set my watch. The ubiquitous red double-decker bus traced the popular streets of London as I insisted on sitting on the open-air upper deck, ducks in a cold and wet fog.

A swift commuter bus took us across the countryside to Oxford where we watched the snow gather and the people rush about indefatigably. Lovely and old defines the scenery. We huddled in a pub, eating bubbles and squeek until a bus pulled up for the return trip to Victoria Station.

Not one gym or one bodybuilder did we see in the greater London districts, although four rare characters in shorts were running for the sake of running. Nor did we see a proliferation of overweight, undermuscled and unconditioned citizenry. The folks were almost athletic in their rapid walking from place to place, upstairs and downstairs, darting from train to train, crossing bustling streets, chasing the tube and meeting schedules.

So, we shifted into high gear to keep up with the crowds and play this British game. We never walk at the pace the English walk because in the America we know, we'd look too weird, but it feels good. Once they get where they're going (wherever that is, another mystery), they slow down and relax: chat, read the paper or a book, snooze or muse.

Something else: they have good food available in abundance if you ain't broke, but they don't serve up the best meals in the world. Lotsa sweet breads and fried stuff and beer. Perhaps the facts that protein is in every meal and they don't eat gluttonously keep the Brits from tubbing out.

There's freedom in simplicity. The Royal Lesson here is to keep moving and don't pig out.

ASSOCIATION OF OLDETIME BARBELL AND STRONGMEN

The 24th Annual Association of Oldetime Barbell and Strongmen Awards Dinner has come and gone. The voracious Saturday event, which hungrily consumes a juicy arm and leg of Friday and Sunday, was a strong success. The gang was all there, and then some. They shook hands, hugged and laughed, reflected and reminisced in the hallways and lobbies and lounges of the Marriott in Saddle Brook, New Jersey.

Groups gathered, telling tales and slapping backs. Pieces of iron in shapes of horseshoes or spikes or rebar mysteriously appeared amid small circles of benders, to be reshaped into hearts or coils or twisted art. Groans, oohs and ahs were generously exchanged.

Pat Povilaitis politely approached me one evening as we exited the hotel for a late dinner. Pat, a 30-some friend of a friend who bends and tears unimaginable things for fun, offered to reshape a pair of horseshoes into matching hearts, personally, there on the spot. Not to be outdone, Greg Matonick bent a quarter in his teeth (twice), which proudly sits on my desk next to a broken Ticonderoga #2 pencil.

I broke the pencil.

The gang is comprised of old-time strongmen and their wives and friends and fans and enthusiasts. And they're all characters. The dinner originated as physical culturist Vic Boff's party honoring Sig Klein, an early NYC gym owner, a quarter of a century ago. It's become an annual tradition and has grown in popularity, substance and significance over the years.

To be honorably added to the honorable list of honorees is a true honor and I am truly honored.

Being thusly credited does not necessarily mean one is old. In fact, the event was the biggest collection of kids outside, perhaps, an overcrowded city high school, a rock concert or a Giant's baseball game. Gray haired, balding, arthritic children wearing eyeglasses and occasionally carrying a cane gathered enthusiastically and peacefully. Hugs, praises, tough-guy handshakes and slaps on backs. No riots, rock throwing or arrests.

It's that way worldwide among guys and gals who associate with the iron and steel and muscles and might. I think it has something to do with osmosis and molecular activity, density and gravity, pursuit and persistence, sanity and insanity, hope, love and good will.

Coming into town for the event, we arrived in our packed-to-the-rack aircraft at Newark International late Thursday night. Our luggage did not. Swell! I feel like I've seen this flick before.

We rented an aerodynamic hydrocarbon-powered eco-vehicle (Jeep SUV) and were off and into the east coast night. My co-pilot followed the GPS and I followed my nose and we arrived at our Saddle Brook digs some 30 minutes northwest about two hours later. We laughed all the way, hunger, frustration and weariness our delightful companions.

No food, too late. Tuna and protein powder locked safely in the lost luggage. Nearest fast food was in the Bahamas. A day of sitting, flying and driving has us limping, squinting and squealing. We crash before our luck runs out.

We eat breakfast in our room like wounded patients in rehab. Our luggage arrives before too long, and we act as if we've been reunited with long-lost friends. The carefully prepared items, our fancy going-to-the-grand-ball wardrobe, is tangled and knotted like the rags they are. The Homeland Security pest-control has been busy at work!

The whitish powder in the tampered zip-lock baggy (protein powder) has managed to emerge as a light dust everywhere, and the innocuous cans of high-protein tuna have been intensely scrutinized (I'm guessing here).

No bombs, no WMD, no assault rifles.

Restored, revitalized and rejuvenated, we take the elevator to the lobby...where the fun begins. I'm about as social as a moon dweller, but I'm also willing to jump out of trees to access the ground. On three, the elevator door opens and there's Lou Mezzanotte, an old training cohort of Laree's from Maryland's famous Dynamo Barbell Club, circa 1984. He has just arrived and is as hungry as a horse. We're off to the local IHOP for omelets, steaks and eggs.

We also begin to practice our knack for recollecting and socializing.

Once the ice is broken, everyone falls in and the water is fine. The day unfolds like a flowering rosebush, thorns and blooms and fragrances everywhere. The lobby and hallways serve as accidental and spontaneous meeting places. Old acquaintances and new friends congregate in corners and alcoves, and late morning becomes early afternoon. It goes something like this:

A room with chairs seats 50 companionable guys and dolls who share memorabilia and experiences and stories. Another room is arranged with a mic and chalkboard to assist Joe Abbenda, AAU Mr. America of the early 1960s, with his inspiring seminar. Benders of steel, lifters of stones and men who defy the physics of gravity and molecular bonding perform acts for encouraging and awed audiences by the outdoor pool.

"Splish splash, I was bending a spike while balancing a round, 230-pound polished granite stone on the back of my neck."

I miss lunch (sorry, we close at 2:00) and go to the room for a can of albacore and a stiff shot of protein powder. My socializing mechanism is smoking and needs to be cooled and refueled. I return later in the afternoon to find things accelerating and escalating. There's the tall guy in black with no fat who's split countless tons of quarry rock for 50 years...with a sledgehammer. Don't mess with Slim, the Hammerman. He has hammers for hands and appreciates respect.

We're buddies, Slim and me.

A young publisher, Del Reddy, greets me and hands me a copy of his recent-most work, *Mr. Weightlifting.* It's the incredible story of heavyweight Olympic and World Champion, Norbert Schemansky. And it's autographed to me. Wow! He's a hero.

Joe Rollino was a wiry fellow who looked every minute of 75—amiable, not shy, skits around the crowds like a firefly and was loved by everyone. He was also 102 years old. That would be 37 years older than me. He bent quarters in his teeth...I got one.

Funny thing: When someone that old is alive and walking and talking, you want to grab him and shake him and hug him. So I did.

Dinner is on time, offering the standard fare of chicken or fish, and the guests sit at round tables of 10 or 12 in front of the straight length of table arranged for the officials and guests of honor. I sit between Fred Yale, my personal introductionist, and Mike Karchut, an amazing Olympic lifter of the '60s and '70s, also being honored.

We three are cut from the same block and friendship was easy.

Artie Drecshler, weightlifting coach and author and special super-guy, leads the whole affair. John Davis is the inspiring posthumous honorarium. Various entertainment is presented throughout the dinner, including the awards. The people are wonderful, their conversations electrifying, and the energy contagious.

I want the award, a distinguished walnut and brass plaque, and the stunning 12x18 painting of me by noteworthy artist Jim Sanders, but I don't want to stand before the crowd and speak. I'll wet my pants. Just pass them over to me and I'll smile broadly and be on my way.

This was not acceptable, so I fashion a comfortable conversation that includes my early weightlifting beginnings, my dull and eventless life, and my most current days…a little history in a nutshell. Ugh, but it'll have to do.

I practice it, I envision, I imagine. I'm ready.

Fred Yale, a swell guy, spends 10 minutes introducing me with professionalism and precision. Absolutely everything I was going to say, he says, and better. I'm wiped out, not a detail left, nothing.

They carry me off in a basket.

SACRAMENTO INVADED BY MUSCLEBOUND AMBASSADORS

How we got here is a long story, so please don't ask.

We sat in the sweeping balcony of the Capitol Building's ornate Senate Chamber, Frank and Christine Zane, Penny and Dick Tyler (*West Coast Bodybuilding Scene*), Ann and Peter McGough (*Flex* and *Muscle & Fitness* senior editor) and Laree and me, peering down upon California's finest governmental figures at work, a hardhat area of another sort. It was shortly after noon, when Joe Weider was being officially honored by Governor Schwarzenegger and the State of California: July 9th—the state's new Joe Weider Day.

The family of Joe and Betty Weider was seated in various sections of the gallery, as were official friends of the Governor. Lunch was arranged shortly after the ceremony in the conference room attached to the Governor's office. Security guards, officials and assistants buzzed everywhere like worker bees. None of us in our little muscley group expressed any disappointment that we hadn't pursued public service or government as a career choice.

Even amid the innocuous procedure of awarding an elder citizen for his outstanding contribution to society, the heehaw of politics raised its ugly voice. The Senate Pro Tem introduced the Governor with less-than-amusing acrid remarks about Arnold's presence in the Chamber and the opportunity of meeting "the man responsible for bringing him to America."

Oh, boy!

Not long later, we filed out and made our way to the luncheon, our appetites in our suit coat pockets. The fellow who led us and the fellow who trailed wore shoulder holsters and ear pieces and whispered incessantly to their lapels. We decided at the last moment to abort the attack, cancel the strike and abandon the takeover. There'd be another time.

The room was alive with people of all walks of life, and included cousins, champions, cops, robbers, Sly Stallone, governmental spokespersons, journalists and cameramen. What a feast!

Observation is my forte. I observe well. I'm a better observer than I am a participant. Or, to be candid, I stare dumbly rather than mingle and socialize enthusiastically. One syllable words tumble from my mouth like water from a slow-leaking faucet: hi, yup, er, ah, huh, wha, nope, yup, nope.

Glad-handing, casual introductions and dutiful sound bites filled the animated room for 30 minutes. My deep and influential conversation with Melissa Johnson, the Executive Director of the President's Council on Physical Fitness, was interrupted at one point, when I was handed a mic and positioned swiftly before the roving video camera: "Say something to Joe Weider."

Spontaneously, unhesitatingly, excitedly, I drew upon my insight and powers of articulation. Huh, um, yup, as we all know, Mr. Weider, The Trainer of Champions, otherwise, Joe, far be it from me, er…furthermore. My lips sizzled with inspiration and authority and newly cast words never before spoken on the planet earth: reamazible, extramarketorial, supravisionish.

I was impressive, indeed. My eyes darted about like a pair of guppies looking for a secret way out of the bowl.

Everyone settled down and assumed their seats after catching up and making new acquaintances. We ate a light lunch of tasty chicken salad as the roundtable socializing continued. The Terminator, seated five feet to my right between Rocky and the Master Blaster, regularly received 4x6 cards informing him of news updates and the latest events in Chambers, which he discreetly scrutinized and calmly managed. I, the Bomber, was alert and ready with any advice or assistance he might need.

Arnold spoke, Franco spoke, Melissa spoke, and Joe was honored.

A short film was shown depicting Joe Weider's remarkable rags-to-riches life—borrowed-nickels to multi-billions, major development of bodybuilding and staggering influence on the health and fitness history. We applauded sincerely. The guy built the ship, raised the sails, manned the helm and set the course, his hands alone. He managed the winds and rough seas, endured the still air and silent waters and negotiated rocky reefs and uncharted oceans. No one showed him the way.

The luncheon wound down in a timely fashion and the guests were offered a private tour of the Capitol Building. We opted to locate our nearby hotel to take advantage of some quiet time. The heat of Sacramento laid its heavy hand on our brow, and the uncommon activities pulled at our ear, while the special attire caused tugging, itching and hives.

How does Arnold do it?

Evening came right on time, and Team Draper made our way to Lucca, the favorite eating place of the local political emissaries. We walked the six blocks with Frank and Christine Zane and Bill Chatfield, the energetic Director of the Selective Service System. After a block, I began to fall behind, which is deadly to the ego of winged warriors. I managed each step carefully and seriously to accommodate my less-than-quick-and-sturdy, post-bypass gait.

Confessing my mortality and apologizing for my temporarily weakened state, the subject of heart surgery became the center of conversation for Bill and me. Later, Dick Tyler, a 30-year-veteran of chiropractic medicine and the renowned author of *West Coast Bodybuilding Scene,* hooked up with Bill at dinner and entered a passionate hour-long conversation, heads together and ignoring their tablemates. Fascinating!

The guests at Lucca, a new restaurant with lots of atmosphere and wood and open street-front windows, congregated in a private garden patio. Drinks were served and we proceeded to further our friendships—the same faces minus the diplomatic types, with fewer whispering men-in-black. Name cards placed judiciously on the single long table designated the seating arrangement.

The lights were dimmed as one by one people gave up intermingling and chose the cushioned seats bearing their names. Ah, to sit: Joe Weider at the center of the table with Arnold and Betty to his left; we sat to Joe's right, and the Zanes and Tylers across from the man of the day. What a crew.

Joe was 87 and as in love with bodybuilding as he was 70 years ago when he cranked out his very first muscle publication in his family's front room in Montreal.

Today and tomorrow, the weather and taxes were discussed, evaluated and argued among the Golden Age contemporaries. Mostly, the memories were deep and wide and stirring. We were nice folks, good, grateful and kind. The food was exceptional, a menu offering variety and the best money could buy. Thanks, Joe. Thanks, Arnold.

Intermittent silences indicated the company's undivided attention to eating, savoring and appreciating. Time continued its march unencumbered, and the early departures began.

"Thanks for everything, so good to meet you, you have my number, it was our pleasure, please call, see you again soon and bye-bye."

Frank eased to the front of the table now scattered with half-full glasses of wine and iced tea, his signature harmonica-and-poetry tribute about to unfold. All eyes and ears and rhythmically clapping hands were directed to Mr. Olympia as he celebrated "Weider, Our Leader" one more time. His rich, bluesy harmonica stole the show and his sing-song words, though not Robert Frostesque (nor meant to be), accented his appreciation of Joe Weider. Faces beamed.

Laughter and grins and draining upend glasses…Time to go, guys and girls and you muscle worshippers. The walk back to the hotel was hopeful, visions of soft mattresses and pillows and quietude drifting in our heads.

Home is anywhere you hang your wings.

YOU'VE GOTTA BE KIDDING

It's the third week of February, a month before a fabulous spring. How do I know that, you ask, these and other things equally scintillating and profound? I'm an official timekeeper, an important post by which I am honored. I have a calendar hanging on the wall, a clock on my desk and a precise hour glass strategically situated on a nearby utility shelf. Very professional, very efficient.

I also do the weather (it's pretty nice out) and give traffic reports (the freeway's a mess) and make up facts about almost anything that comes to my mind—baby dogs are also called adorable puppies, standing barbell curls build neat muscles, squats are really hard, and on and on.

These duties plus my workouts keep me busy, leaving little time for recreation. My single pastime has been hanging around waiting for inspiration to write a weekly column. Of course, inspiration is not always forthcoming, whereupon I must resort to invention or improvisation, black magic or pulling my hair out. The hair is going fast.

This week was a tad unlike the rest, an exception, you might say…almost bizarre. I was dozing before my blank computer screen, hypnotized by its pulsing drone, when the phone rang. Who the heck can that be, was my first reaction. Why don't they go away was my second. I picked up after the 10th ring and said with my usual charm, "WHAT?!" She said, "Hi, Mr. Draper," a little song in her voice, and provided me with more stimulus stimulation than I could ever imagine.

The story goes something like this:

A month ago in a column titled, "Health and Strength and the Joys of Living," I grumbled about shortness of breath and a pending visit to a heart doc to assess its origin. How bothersome! Medication or somewhat-non-invasive stent placement were the possible solutions I was expecting. I ain't no dummy. I trained at the Muscle Beach Dungeon, I'm a physical culturist and authentic ironhead.

Well, three heart doctors—cardiothoracic specialists known for their genius, advanced learning and meticulous skills—determined I was close in my suspicions (it's the heart), but not exact in my diagnosis (needs more than aspirin and a good night's rest). Get this: Curly, Moe and Larry, as I have affectionately named the amusing threesome, agreed the best fix is quadruple bypass surgery, "and while we're at it, let's repair that leaky valve. What the heck!"

Rats! Just when I was hitting my mid-60's stride, I thought.

I thanked them for their generous contribution of fodder, my head reeling with dazzling thoughts of the copious writing material I suddenly and unexpectedly had at my disposal.

Good news comes in heaps and piles and quadruplicates.

Have you ever experienced true joy, dear friends?

Here's one of the best parts: As you read this, I'm recovering in postoperative care somewhere in the bowels of a huge, highly reputed hospital in San Jose, California. I'd have told you sooner, but I just found out—it was no emergency, just swift action. I'll be back in the gym before spring, knocking out sets like golf balls at a driving range.

Number two of the many best parts: I'll be as good as new…well, almost new…maybe, slightly used…used, but not broken.

Seriously, the reparations will provide enhanced oxygenation (this translates to improved energy and endurance…step aside), breathing comfort (no horrid gasping) and muscle recovery (huge and ripped), and reduced daily fatigue and post-set exhaustion. The old freight train is moving from the rusty county rails to the shiny interstate express tracks.

Number three: I did not cause the disease of the arteries by my addictive behavior 25 years ago. As the doctor said, "You didn't do this; someone else did." Arteriosclerosis is mostly genetic in my naturally low-cholesterol body. I inherited the vulnerability, though there are no signs of heart disease in my immediate family.

Four, a big relief: It's not contagious.

Finally, I have the opportunity to experience and review the whole catastrophe firsthand and pass on my observations, assuming you're interested.

To this tall tale, I will add the commentaries of the ever-so-clever doctors for scientific flavor.

We're jazzed! Sounds like fun, Draper. Can't wait!

Like, for example, I'm told stuff like four to five days in the hospital for recovery; up and walking the day following surgery and every day thereafter; smoking in parking lot only (joke); no movement or exercise that will cause stress on the repairing sternum (an eight-week process), meaning no flys, pullovers, bench presses, hysterics, giggling or uncontrolled laughter.

Grimacing is permissible. It seems it's the mending of the sternum, not the heart, that requires time and prevents desperate muscleheads like me from tossing the iron within a day or two of the incisions.

I imagine there will be pain (how loud can I scream MORE MORPHINE, MAXINE?) and I'll feel as sick as a dog for a few days. Then the impatience will spill from my guts and frustration and discouragement will penetrate the marrow of my bones. At the feet of these towering challenges, I shall grow stronger, while simultaneously devising ways of training without undoing the good the doctors have so skillfully done.

It is written that through the eye of a needle a camel can pass if he tries real hard...slightly paraphrased, incidentally.

I have sardines and tuna under my hospital pillow and an iPod loaded with my favorite tunes (Kate Smith, The McGuire Sisters, The Mills Brothers, Lawrence Welk, Ink Spots).

Until this day, I've never touched an iPod, for your information. It's this kind of information you'll be receiving regularly now that I'm a Quipee (quad patient). Provocative, entertaining, cutting edge—no pun intended.

Other good things coming from my downtime in addition to the pump repair is the overdue layoff to rest the rickety joints and dilapidated body systems under load for a long, long time. I shall bask in thankfulness as the days gently roll by, nibbling beef jerky and listening to the scintillating sounds of the great Tony Bennett and Vaughn Monroe.

Gratitude, a sleeping giant, shall be awakened and revisited, as I grasp the truth that life goes on, and not without me.

I proposed to the doctors that perhaps they could perform a tummy tuck while I'm under sedation…remove the loose skin under my chin. No soap! They're a stiff bunch.

I'm fine, though I find gliding less fulfilling than soaring, landings less challenging than takeoffs. Don't taxi when you can fly…and when you can fly, fly high.

Post Note: I hope you realize I joke about my choice of music.

TOO EARLY FOR INSIGHT

My plump and uncertain fingers descend upon the keyboard, the first time in 15 days, as many days since my hands have grasped the weights causing them to clang and struggle for release. I don't miss the weights; they're objects of interest for healthier and stronger men than I. But I do miss you, the objects of my affection.

To set your mind at ease from the beginning, the surgical procedure went well and I'm recovering. Each day is better than the last. Some days I wish I were dead, others I think I'm going to die. Some days I laugh, some days I cry.

I'm home now, the hospital to my back, and I'm adjusting a light that appears to be the end of a long and echoing tunnel.

I'll make this note short, leaving the details to another day, a more lucid mind and hands more nimble than hooks on a hoist. Because here's the thing: I'm tired.

I'll not yet dramatize the bleakness of open-heart surgery, the smiles going in and the freakiness coming out (the experience is yet to be completed), and instead ponder with you some of the highlights that dance across my mind.

For example, did you know hospitals are open and running all night long? They're busy in every corridor with doors slamming, beds traveling in different directions like barges on a delta; commands are delivered with a harsh compassion and every article—dolly, bottle, tube, dressing, needle, pill, message—is sterilized, scrutinized and passed on from one pair of skilled hands to the next.

Nurses rule where no creatures go. The sounds come in waves like sounds in a big city with the rhythmic cycle of bedside checkups, regular applications of medications, whispered reactions to every detail, hushed responses to every query and sign-language evaluations for each urgency.

Where have all the cowboys gone? They've become nurses.

Nurses speak every tongue under the sun: men and women, short and tall, colors to match a rainbow, personalities of every description and indefatigable. How they do what they do without exploding absolutely mystifies me. They leave in the morning and return again at night and start the whole thing over again. They have names like Mary, Jane, Yen, Raffy, Barbara, Evelyn, Chu and Anna. They're heroes!

I arrived at Good Sam's Pre-surgical Admitting at 5:15 a.m. for my quadruple bypass and valve procedure. It's as dark as hell at that hour, and the fires were blazing.

It wasn't long before I was registered and in a gown, parked outside the sparkling operating room marked, Surgical B. Nurses, doctors and attendants roamed the halls of the inner sanctum, occasionally stopping by to say hello and offer a comforting word.

"I'm fascinated by the activity and equipment and preparations," I told the anesthesiologist as she reviewed my charts. I said nothing of the fact that I wanted to go home (now), and I had just wet my pants.

I thought of the gang and knew you were with me, wanted me to be strong and fly high. The team rolled me in as I knew they would. "Hi, everybody," was my greeting, accompanied by a contrite smile.

The truth is, I was confident in the doctors, hopeful in the Lord, the Almighty, and 60 seconds from disappearing into the oblivion of some powerful drug...99, 98, 97, 9-.

I returned to planet earth in 13 million pieces about 10 hours later. All the nice people were gone and I was alone with a pack of vicious hellions. The pain was not like any pain I've known.

It hurt my soul, confused my mind and threatened my existence.

The ICU nurses didn't believe me. I couldn't breathe. They didn't care. I knew what to do and how to fix it, but they didn't listen. They looked past me; I prompted, I provoked, I hissed.

There was a tube down my throat, a ventilator, to regulate my breathing. In regulating my breathing, it also prevented my speaking. This turned out to be my greatest horror—instant verbal communication gone. All other pain was mere discomfort, a joy in comparison. I desperately sought understanding and was at every turn told, NO, loud and clear.

I was never so deeply affected by anything.

I worked my way through the haze and maze slowly, ever so slowly, until the nasty gadget was removed. From that moment, life loomed before me like a flock of wild geese straining across the cold, early morning winter sky, ugly bats outta hell.

Tonight, post-op day 13, I'll dig into our digs and watch the evening bump around. I'm getting better, they say. War stories can get old fast, especially telling them as they unfold. We've been busy with little things that have become momentarily, temporarily big: sitting, standing, lying; don't cough, never sneeze.

I'm swollen everywhere (19-inch calves—hellooo), have shortness of breath (most miserable), get the chills and spinouts and walk as I'm able, all of which brings me to the end of my narrow runway.

OMS (One Might Say): Be strong and courageous.

TIME FLIES WHEN YOU'RE HAVING FUN

I've done my share of complaining this week. I prefer to call it meaningful observation with a touch of drama to provide in-the-moment authenticity. It might be whimpering, sniveling and grotesque. Eighteen days since the good doctor made the first incision, and I'm on the mend.

The days are long, not predictable, colored in tones of gray, demanding and rancid. They're also laced with hope and relief, insight and gratitude. I'm not alone in my little journey and the email from all corners of world remind me of this comforting truth.

To ease my mind—becoming overwhelmed when recovering from open-heart surgery is common and destructive, and should be handily avoided—allow me to thank you supporting me during these unusual times. Not a prayer, get-well wish, graceful thought, good vibe, hearty encouragement, candle lighting or positive meditation has gone unnoticed, and is deeply appreciated. Through them we, you and us, are becoming bigger, stronger and faster.

Now about my scars: I have three beauties. One goes down the belly of the left forearm for 12 inches and it's oozy. From that incision, they harvested an artery. A vein was retrieved from the 13-inch slice on the inside of the right thigh. It's crooked and almost healed. Down the center of the sternum is a clean and well-behaved 10-inch zipper that's, oddly, the least nasty of the trio. The experts promise they'll heal nicely and in time be faint memories.

Here's a funny thing about the less-than-lovely invasive cuts across my hard-worked, once-polished body: I adjusted to them immediately.

How the doctors have the nerve to inscribe the bloody things I'll never know, nor shall I ponder deeply.

Next subject, please.

The kitchen counter is a functional display of bandages, remedies and open drug containers. There's something for everything: pain, blood thinning, blood clotting, inflammation, stool softening (cute), water retention, hiccups, infection and bad cholesterol. With a dozen different medications swirling around the body and mind, I might get confused and gobble them like Red Hots. It's a temporary load until the system regroups, identifies itself and requires a more basic concoction of Western medicine.

I'm mostly listless and the gym is far away. Curiously, I am well adjusted to these facts of life. The fatigue will give way to desire as I heal, the energy will return when it has completed its work in the major repair process, and the gym will resume its intimate place without anxiety or undue haste. The surgeon said I was run over by a trailer truck; it stopped abruptly and backed over me, and then proceeded forward with a roar just to be sure.

I get the picture: fresh road kill.

I'm up one minute and down the next…or is it the other way around? Progress is counted step by step, often intentionally, and savored. It works, this positive reinforcement. I ate, took my pills, went to the bathroom, bathed, made two important phone calls, got my blood test, walked…Good boy and a pat on the head for you.

And then I'm a mess. This is not uncommon, depression, the origins of which are numerous, logical and not extraordinary: itchy-scratchy discomfort, pain from a dozen sources, congestion, swelling, out of breath, confused and restless. A cascade! It's worse at night; fatigue takes over, darkness crowds, and sleep, an elusive character, paces in the shadows of the mind.

Mornings are always a fresh new start, even though the nights are a bear. My sunrise smile is as big as my prayer for another day—a good day, thank you, God. Bears growl, but they're beautiful animals.

Open-heart patients are awarded two gifts at the outset of operations: a small pillow and a plastic gadget resembling a sterile, high-tech bong pipe. The pillow is offered with reverence and declared unmistakably by doctor, nurse and former suffering patients to be your best friend; it should not be absent, misplaced or out of reach. It seems any active stirring within the chest cavity—clearing the throat, grunting, coughing, hiccupping, sneezing—projects pressure on the newly set and wired sternum, causing pain that's off the charts. Rolling up the soft object and holding it against the sternum tightly counters the forceful bursts and prevents unmentionable agony.

That pillow is forgotten only once.

The clear plastic gizmo is a breath-measuring device commercially called a Voldyne. It's also a tool to be used regularly to exercise the lungs, restore their function and improve their capacity. You bite on a tube attached to the simple ruled gauge and inhale and exhale five times with all your might. The inhale determines your prize. Throughout the day, this procedure (it becomes a ritual) is practiced, and outdoing yourself workout by workout becomes the goal. Does that sound familiar? I do five sets of five reps five times a day, 5x5x5, seven days a week.

I'd rather be curling.

Since starting my erratic tapping on the keyboard only yesterday to convey these post-op thoughts, I've taken another giant step forward in mood, energy, painfree-ness and hope. We're later to buzz around town to accomplish errands and keep me on my toes. The appetite is coming back, and I weighed 212 this morning.

Walking will suffice as my hardcore exercise, though I just got the urge to formulate some sort of daily routine to stretch and stimulate the muscles hanging from my bones. These are very good signs to the captain of a lost and distressed craft. The sun shining outside the open doors is a big help, and last night I slept almost seven hours straight.

Thankful is the number one feeling.

I look down and consider the bare evidence (literally) of my adventure. Humility is the number two feeling on my list. Stooped, shallow and pale, scarred, bruised and swollen. What a mess, I think with a grin. This, too, will pass as I, along with you, move forward and onward. I'll leave the lumps and bumps behind and carry with me only the newly acquired equipment that makes life less difficult, more understandable and more precious, richer, sweeter and deeper.

We live, we learn, we grow.

Now this is peculiar: I became so preoccupied with the doctors and hospitals and surgery and pain and recovery and details that I totally forgot the original purpose and consequence of the whole catastrophe: the successful repair of a diseased and broken heart, and the incomparable goodness that accompanies it. The rubies and gold were overshadowed by crude, dense lead and shards of dull glass.

Enough wallowing, it's time to rejoice!

DAY 25 AND COUNTING

Twenty-five days after I was harpooned by a skilled cardio-thoracic surgeon, I dragged my stinky gym bag from the closet. I was headed for the gym and needed it for security, not for its contents: thick leather lifting belt, heavy duty knee and wrist wraps, a Top Squat, DMSO. Heavy-duty and thick were not part of today's plan. I simply wanted to enter the hallowed iron halls, take a deep breath and nibble at the edges of the equipment.

I was more curious than hungry.

My trusty gym bag weighed a ton. Collars, chain, tuna, water bottle, selected tools, lubricants...they all add up and come in handy when you least expect them to. A brief inspection to identify my belongings indicated a mouse had taken up residence in the main compartment of the bag. A half-eaten protein bar lay in the corner amid shreds of foil wrapping. Further, the shreds were arranged neatly to form a cozy nook, a shelter from the elements. Less than a month, and already I was displaced, evicted, tossed on the streets, homeless.

I snatched the food supply and makeshift fortification from the bag and scoured the adjacent areas for contraband. A wrist strap had chunky bites wrenched from its side, more material for the snug winter dwelling place. All I needed was Godzilla the Mouse moving into my territory. My newly repaired heart skipped a beat.

Laree was behind the wheel and we were off to the gym before we could change our minds. It's not wise to drive while recovering from open-heart surgery, as the freshly dissected sternum is vulnerable to direct steering wheel impact should an accident occur. Good point.

Zoom, zoom!

This sunny Sunday afternoon, the gym was spotted with three other muscleheads with no place to go. My energy level has not been good, going from rotten to lousy to crummy over the slow days of recovery. I expected as much, and thank God I'm alive. However, as I climbed the steps to the gym's back door, an old-time feeling slid into place, like a greasy gear in an old Chevy transmission. The place was as fresh and friendly as yesterday, same music, same slanting sunshine and shadows, same swell smell, same clink and clang.

Home!

I grabbed my water and headed for the leg press, first things first.

My legs have been wobbly since exiting the hospital. Jelly quads have a way of reducing one to a defenseless heap; everything is uphill and a mile away. And if boogiemen chase you, you can't run.

The first set was very nice. Feet well-placed, ample oxygenation, the steel platform went up and down for 20 reps, just as prescribed. I huffed and puffed. Another pair of plates was added to the press by my trusty sidekick. I did some calf raises and stretched while regaining my hampered breath. The second set was also very nice, up and down for 20 more reps (10, pause, 5, pause and 5). The thighs felt strong and solid, though the endurance was severely limited.

That's where time and patience and courage come into play, I assured myself with a deep voice of authority.

The third set was accomplished with three plates on each side. I totaled 15 reps and felt the weight bearing down on my twig-like limbs. One more set? After careful consideration, much gasping and a glare from the captain, I decided instead to knock off four sets of leg extensions with some dinky calf raises thrown in for good measure. The reps were strong, effective and had a graceful rhythm to them.

I've been here before.

I know what you're saying: "Give the bomber a match and he wants the whole stick of dynamite. He'll never learn, and he proposes to teach us? Blast yourself into oblivion, Nutso!"

Thanks, I needed that. I'm tempted, but tempered. No way shall I step too close to the edge of exertion and look down its long and lonely descent. I've been there before too.

Walking to the next general location of useful equipment was no rounded-back shuffle. I stepped with purpose and a revived gait. So what it was a pair of 15-pound dumbbells that held my interest? They felt like a ton! Time for some curls—seated dumbbell alternates—to awaken the sleeping dwarfs hanging by my sides.

I had no idea if the weights would move simply because I willed it. They were under dubious control; an incision that resembled a stretch of barbed wire on the forearm led to a boney hand like a trowel (its partner, a rake), a dehydrated body still swimming in a stew of mixed chemicals and a mind as questioning as a two-year-old's...Why's the sky blue?

The dumbbells rose without hesitation—left, then right—with precision and remarkable ease...until the 10th rep, where a wall stood firmly in place. I panted, raised the weight by five and did 10 more solid beauties. After three delightful sets, I turned my nose to pulley pushdowns, and wondered if the muscle recruitment and torso flexing would present a problem. Nope. Not with a sensible weight and every sensor engaged.

My arms, wispy stems of a bush, rejoiced.

The seated lat row is situated conveniently at the low end of the dumbbell rack. How could I resist?

I adjusted the weight stack to a laughable number and gave her a tug. Joke's on me; the weight wouldn't budge with the force I was willing to exert. I'm not proud, no one is looking and I just had surgery, after all. I lowered the weight and got three sets of 10 with full range of motion, a squint of pain in the clavicle (easy, boy!) and a minor pump in the lower back.

I'm grateful, bordering on ecstatic.

Shoulders. Something for shoulders. Can't press in this condition. How about one-arm lateral raises to the side while holding onto a support post and leaning slightly outward? I had just rediscovered this movement before my visit to Good Sam's and it was very tasty. Now, I can't say until I put it into action. Iffy!

Ten pounds is enough to determine its worth. The little dumbbell went upward, in the right track and the full distance with a light contraction at the peak for good measure. It came down as it went up, very well…you might say swell.

Laree's looking on as if I'd cleaned and pressed 315. "You mean that doesn't tear at your seams? This is wild," she said. I did the big three of 10 reps, working up to the hulky 20-pounder. Look out, stand back, coming through, heads up.

I finished with the Hammer chest press, three sets of 20, with small change on the machine's yolks. This surprised me because the sternum is exactly in the middle of the conflict, but I achieved full range of motion without splitting in half or feeling like I was scalded with a hot iron. No undue stress. Wow!

And then we walked to the car and drove home. Shower, food, fireplace and the beat of time.

I was encouraged. The next day, I drove to the gym myself (look out, wildlife) to do what I didn't do the first time around. Crunches, thumbs-up curls supersetted with machine dips, which I didn't expect to even consider for six months. It appears to be a direct assault on wired sternums and relieved pectoral muscles. But... no problemo with a light weight and 50 years of practice, then a resourceful two-handed cable movement resembling a dumbbell pullover (stimulating), one-arm cable lat row, widegrip bar-to-chin pulldown and another round with the hammer chest press.

Three sets of 10s and 12s and I'm happy—not with me, but the range of exercises with fair exertion and no threatening pain or limiting action.

Alternating left and right sides of the muscle groups where doable is smart way to exercise when considering the heart's load and overload. Divide the exertion, focus on the action, enjoy the engagement.

Light weights are fun and high reps have their heated moments and both can save a body from a terrible crunching. Repair and restoration revive involvement and discovery.

After a beating, you enter the gym and look from the sensible end of the telescope, not the end that indicates where you were and what you did before the whoopin,' but the end that reminds you when you couldn't reach for a glass of water or whisper your best friend's name.

The tough times and the good times—the real times—are lining up like dominoes.

THUNDER AND LIGHTNING, SUNSHINE AND RAINBOWS

It was seven years ago when a good friend of ours went to the doctor for his annual physical, a requirement of his employer. A big man and solid as a rock from powerlifting most of his life, he dropped by the clinic as prescribed. His vital statistics were alarming for a man just 50, an emergency angiogram was ordered, and he was sent to surgery for a multiple bypass before he being released toward home a week later.

Now Tom is a brave guy; he recovered fully and was that weird kind of grateful one experiences after a nick-of-time discovery. He also made it clear to his friends and colleagues that what goes on behind one's walls of flesh is not always harmonious and good and right. Jarring and bad and wrong is often the case. Beware. Be aware. Get checked up and checked out.

I took his words of experience seriously, and because of my own shortness of breath, arranged an angiogram with my heart doctor. I was fitted with two stents and was made increasingly aware of my heart's needs and vulnerability. But, as it turns out, that episode was not to be the end of it.

I like to think we have a long and eventful journey before us. Now to unloose myself of the chains that bind me. Spend too much time with doctors and clinics and prescription drugs and you begin to feel—and act—like a professional patient.

I have a few friends who operate in such a zone, half their lives are spent arranging doctors' appointments, reapportioning medications, treks to the pharmacy and filling out disability and insurance forms. The other half is creatively expended inventing new dilemmas, locating new doctors, complaining about their various ailments and dismally recuperating from them all.

The art of being sick and depressed is loathsome, and it is not dying. The art of living is worth developing.

It's been four weeks since the surgeon handily performed an arterial switcheroo—healthy blood passageways from my left arm and right leg transferred to ailing heart regions, anterior and posterior. Subsequent visits to doctors' offices confirm I'm on the road to recovery, bumping along for the ride and behaving like a model patient. I've repeatedly topped out the Voldyne breathing meter at 5,000ml, its highest register, up from 1,500 in the early post-op days…a lifetime ago.

I'm a regular bag of wind.

I've made it through my third, fourth and fifth post-surgical workouts with increasing energy and strength. I supersetted comfortably, naturally contracted the muscles more intensely and sought each set with more spirit and song.

My recuperation throughout the days was marked. I didn't go home and collapse, but instead did chores around the house, including laundry and vacuuming. (The kitchen remodel and house-painting will have to wait until the end of the month.)

My appetite is hardy, but the bodyweight is down. I'm a rail, taking diuretics to combat the water retention common to open-heart surgery. Diuretics drain energy as well as water from your system. Ugh! Sleep is a battle, hot sweats waking me frequently and causing discomfort—another post-op downer.

I'll regain my weight slowly and certainly, looking at 215 lithe pounds as my new standard. Lithe sounds cool, dontcha think… better than skinny? Two-one-five has not been an effort to maintain in the past, and feels naturally comfortable.

The challenge will be in gaining and sustaining the muscle without milk products. It's been a month since I've had milk, cottage cheese or yogurt—my life-long staples—and the mucus, a life-long problem, is down significantly. Elation!

Furthermore, with genetically impaired arteries, I can do without the added milk fats. I miss the protein and carbs and other associated nutrients, and I miss the good taste. Some will argue that milk is downright bad for you. I'm on the fence between the cow pastures and the marketplace.

Protein powder gets mixed with water and juice and I'm a happy musclebuilder.

Coincidentally, I've adjusted my meat intake downward over the past year, a wise move for an older and less active and less muscle-making creature-machine. Fish of all sorts have become more appealing. I now have lean meat a few times a week, half my usual consumption.

Too much dense LDL and not enough HDL have caught my attention. I'll soon slip into my new bike shoes and go for a spin. Won't that be fun? It's a bird; it's a plane; it's the closet spin biker.

It's still too early for a training plan, though an every-other-day system seems reasonable and likeable. I'll seek balance, control exertion and select exercises as I evaluate the gym and the pulsing vessel standing in its midst. Joy will attract me, intelligence will guide me, understanding will fulfill me, pain will signal me…and fear will leave me.

Socrates might say, know thyself and trust thyself. I say thank God every day.

It's warm and sunny and a day after yesterday's super workout. I'm not sore or whooped from my recent iron encounters since the bombing, swift kicks in the pants that felt better than a hearty slap on the back from an old friend. Today I'll just walk, up and down a long, gradual 100-yard incline that is our driveway. It's springtime; the birds will sing and I'll get the urge to run. Naturally, I'll fight the obsessive urge as my lungs squeal like little piggies hungry for mom's tasty milk. Today's walk will be longer than the last, and more savory.

The insights gained from a post-bombing experience point out the basics with more clarity and give them the importance they deserve and often lose when seen and spoken of again and again. Redundancy beats the life from a good thing.

Tomorrow is another good day.

YOU WIN, YOU LOSE, YOU CRAWL

Seldom do I drag myself to the gym unwillingly. It's not often I stand in front of a barbell or dumbbells with drooping shoulders and hesitation.

And though I don't feel like Superman, never do I question why I'm about to fatigue myself and inflict hard work and pain upon my body. That's all behind me and has been for a long, long time. Today, I roll out the ole Harley, run a cloth over the chrome, crack the pipes and let 'er rip.

This all began lo those long years ago.

I remember when I was a kid—no problem, the weights were playthings. You push, pull, toss, lift and grunt. Great fun. Clank, rattle; where's my wrench? As a teen, lifting was like a sport you played; you win, you lose, the days came and went and skipping a workout was no big deal. Let's see, should I lift weights or play stickball at the park?

One day—who remembers when; it's all a haze—I noticed guilt had taken up residence in my ever-present shadow, a nagging, smirking wise guy—a jerk, really—that made me irritable when I missed a workout, miserable if I was delinquent a week.

Training became a thing I had to do, and the fun was leaking away. Almost anything became more desirable than the weights; studying Latin, changing the oil or cleaning the garage.

Thank heaven there was no TV. I pressed on.

Then some raggedy habit took form and the walk to the weight room became regular, and labored and cheerless. It's lonely on this bench, under this bar and counting sets and reps. How many do I have to do today? The number was a pain in my head, and completing the prescribed task before me was a dull feat.

"Will the workout ever end?" was my approach. The color around me was gray.

This must be done, press on.

It wasn't long before anticipation, the kind with a sour puss, started hanging around with guilt. Put these two thugs together and we have tension, nervous tension. Now it's not only hard work and lonely under the bar, it's tiresome and exhausting thinking about it, all day, at work, at lunch, on the road and in the sack.

By the time I got to the gym, I'd been there, I'd done that. Not another rep! I'm beat. Push that iron.

Swell, but that's not enough.

Besides feeling guilty for missing a workout I haven't missed and badgered by a workout I haven't hit, I'm feeling disappointed with the progress I haven't made. A mob is gathering in my shadow and I'm just a skinny kid. We have Guilty Gus, Big Al Anticipation and the notorious Duke of Disappointment conspiring in the dark. Step aside, mutts, I'm using that squat rack.

Duty calls when you're still and listen to your soul. Taking the three pot-bellied bums down became my mission and I knew it—the first sign of instinct, survival of the fittest, which plays no minor role in the muscle-builder's life. Instinct rules.

In this life you win, you lose or you crawl. It's not that I wanted to win, but I cannot lose and I will not crawl. Elementary, really, and I worked by elimination. I gathered from their focus on me that what I was focused on was very important and very good because they're so bad. Despite, or because of, the combined efforts of the gloomy threesome, I pressed on.

Then I discovered devotion and intensity.

Strangely, my shadow grew larger with my body and the three wise guys grew smaller. In time, I replaced guilt with discipline, a stern but agreeable character. Negative anticipation submitted to positive preparation and psyching up, a pair of confident spirits with lofty goals.

And disappointment, sour and ungrateful, left one fine day without a word. Like mistakes, the scoundrels taught tough lessons. Their departure was an unconscious relief, dirty snow and slippery ice slowly melting in the spring.

The walk to the gym became hurried, not soon enough, and excitement accompanied my footsteps. Miles were behind me and miles were ahead and somehow I knew the way. You never know the way unless you walk it and climb it, get lost, lose ground, grow cold, hungry and insist on walking again.

Nobody can tell you, exactly, what, how and why; they can only offer their hopeful presence, wise suggestions and solid encouragement—gold ore and uncut diamonds.

My word, what's the big deal? It's only lifting weights; it's exercise and good food. It's not life, liberty and the pursuit of happiness.

So now where am I—where are we—in my recollections? When did the pleasure of training settle in my bones?

When I stepped back and realized its worth; when I resumed doing it for its adventure and immediate reward; when I trusted its permanence; when training was no longer an obligation but a wise choice, a desirable means to eliminate barriers and overcome obstacles and to express myself without screaming for an hour or two, several times a week.

And it's no big ego trip to enjoy physical strength, endurance, reasonable confidence and a body that doesn't resemble a pear balanced precariously on two toothpicks.

There's no more ego than a long list of letters after one's name on a letterhead, a tattoo in the right place, a red Carrera in the driveway, a $1,000 suit or a shaved head.

It took some time, pressed together with considerable doubt, curiosity, pain and some hefty sacrifice to make the discovery, but it was worth it.

To settle into your training with confidence is like sitting back in an easy chair, comfortable and relaxed. Just don't fall asleep on me because we still have work to do—clearing the runway, fueling up, checking the landing gear and struts.

Of course, the choir agrees, and loves to be reminded. How about you, whose t-shirts are getting snug and triceps are forming horseshoes?

Trust, press on toward your sensible goal and put in your time with renewed enthusiasm, because it's happening, and it happens no other way.

Consider how far you've come and imagine—visualize with certainty—where you want to go. The only thing that stands in your way is time and doubt.

Time will pass, but doubt must be removed.

What you need to correct or alter in menu or exercise arrangement, attitude or workout intensity, you will surely attend along the way. Today's questions are tomorrow's answers. Mistakes and injuries are the instructors.

Be strong, keep your sense of humor, stay alert, be positive and hopeful, drink your protein shakes, be nice to your neighbor, squat, of course, and don't ruin your shoulders with heavy bench pressing.

As far as it is possible, allow no unsightly gaps to develop in your eating scheme or your training thrust; they have a way of growing out of control and they are unbearable.

That we are aware of what we must do places us well above the rest.

That we practice what we must puts us on top.

BEHIND THE SMILE

Muscle and Fitness, a colorful and energetic riot of musclemen and musclebuilding information, isn't a recent publication that gained popularity overnight. It has gone by a variety of names over half a century and was reared by a guy named Joe Weider. Joe, dubbed the Trainer of Champions, dragged it from the ink-smeared pages of a manual printing press in his grandma's Montreal apartment, and gave it dramatic life based upon his vision of muscle and might.

I was one of the characters who played a role in his elaborate vision, a Mr. America and Mr. Universe in the dream he presented to the world. Appearing on the scene in the early '60s, I filled the pages of his magazines, adorned their covers and, through inspiring pictures on California beaches, conveyed stories of delight, promise and hope to the young and young at heart.

I smiled broadly, flexed my muscles and frolicked with beach bunnies on lazy, crazy sunny afternoons. The blue Pacific rolled in mightily, billowy clouds with silver linings caressed the horizons and dogs playfully chased seagulls along endless sandy shores. Hop in. The water's fine. Life is grand.

Hold it there. Back up 20 feet and take another look. I see a distressed cameraman and his elaborate gear in a heap of cases, containers and bags; I see a guy—that must be Joe—in half a suit with his sleeves and trouser legs rolled up; off to the side a group of sticky, uninterested bystanders mope about, kick sand and suck on water bottles. These must be the delighted characters in the delightful pictures awaiting a moment of delight.

The sun pours down, hot and relentless, and more baby oil is applied to the muscular bodies. A pump is sought to give vibrancy to fatigued and dehydrated muscles; instead itchy sand is distributed generously to far reaches of the body—ears, eyes, nose and every known crack and crevice. Are we having fun yet?

Now the sun is going down and neither the cameraman nor the subjects can delay the untimely process. Joe is flailing his arms, while Artie Zeller or Russ Warner or Jimmy Caruso—bless their hearts—tries hopelessly to interpret his wild gesticulations. Reflectors are brought in, the location is moved, the ocean grows calm and the dramatic lighting is lost to soft shadows suitable for capturing romance, a bottle of wine and thou. Not good.

But wait! The sun's lowering rays join their own reflection off the ocean's surface and the bodies amid the stunning light are spectacular. Everyone is by some freak of nature in the right spot at the right time and in the right mood. Joe screams at Artie, whose nose is deep in his film bag, to take the picture now, now, now.

Art Zeller was a master photographer and physiques were his specialty. He knows what to do, when and how. The digital camera is not even a dream of the future and, alas, our patient and sensible lensman fusses with his ole' reliable Roloflex. Joe is now tearing at his shirt and performing what appears to be an Indian rain dance and whooping, "Artie, Artie! Shoot the picture! Shoot the picture!"

The pretty models went their way—they could care less for muscleheads in the 1960s—and the muscleheads went theirs. The first thing on their minds was protein and then a workout missed due to the fun and frolic at the beach. But it was worth it, wasn't it? Maybe your mug will be in the mag and you'll be famous. In those days, fame and glory in a muscle magazine and 10 cents got you a cup of coffee.

Hey, buddy, can ya spare a dime?

Undeniably, the most inspiring and pleasant photographic sessions were experienced during the winter. Not! Though snow does not fall, nor the temperatures drop below 50 in southern California, winter is winter is winter. Tis the season for hibernation, losing the tan and gaining weight to accommodate heavy off-season training.

Repair and grow, relax and attend life beyond cuts and striations is the bodybuilder's theme. Let's go to the mountains, the deserts or visit the folks back east. Throw in a few year-end holidays and you've got bulky, round and white all over.

"What's that you say? Pictures on the beach this Saturday? What beach? I thought the beach dried up in the winter, was evacuated, dismantled or closed for repairs."

"An up-coming summer promotion needs to be shot now, Bomber, or I'm out millions of bucks."

Oh! In that case, don't want to lose my $85-a-week shipping clerk's salary. Sure, JW, see ya there… bright and early… I'll bring coffee. The grazing white rhinoceros in Dave Draper's trunks will be me.

I'm training hard, strong as a hippo and about as shapely. Put me on a beach and big-game hunters from miles around will gather to claim me as a trophy. You can't do this, Joe. I'm too young to die. Not the beach. Flash! Cover boy is as white as a blank billboard and twice as big. The only definition I have goes something like this: bulky, rounded, colorless, foolish, unwilling, miserable, pouty.

Breaking News: Unidentified Blimp Hovers Aimlessly Over Southern California Beaches. No Details at This Time.

Smiles form with difficulty on frigid lips. The air is cold and nippy breezes supply shivers in spasms. The unlikely crew of plump and pasty bodies huddles under beach towels to stay warm and protect themselves from blasts of sandy wind. The ocean is ominous, the beach is desolate and surviving seagulls are inland hiding under bushes. Dogs and their owners are home where it's safe and cozy. February is no time for these shenanigans.

Neither is July for that matter.

Joe was quite a character and had more color than a rainbow and twice the gold found at the end. He loved the bodybuilding scene, gave it a stage upon which to play and did more than anyone to present it to the world.

Anyone, that is, except the players themselves. Praise be to musclemen who, driven by passion and desire, did what they did because they had to do it.

The smiles on the beaches were hard-earned and their payment was gained in the dark confines of gyms filled with heavy iron. Barbells were the source of resistance that built the muscles that built the men that built the magazine. I, and the guys before me, lifted the cold and noisy metal not for a moment on a page of paper, but for reasons—wonderful reasons—too numerous to count.

Oh, heck! Let me give it a try. I'll be brief.

There's health, muscle and might for starters. Not bad. There's the fun of lifting weights and the exciting challenge it presents, the physical pushing and pulling and stretching, the intelligent formation of exercises, movements and routines, and the tantalizing pumping, burning and striving. Weight training is a dynamic diversion providing strong camaraderie, identification and hope. Be sure of this: Few pastimes provide more benefits, rewards and fulfillment.

Training builds discipline, perseverance and patience. Mountains are climbed with these superior characteristics, lives are saved and nations are shaped. Tough exercise puts order and rhythm in our lives, diminishing confusion and reducing stress, and that's worth more than a few trips to a psychiatrist's couch. As quality is added to life, so is it extended with useful and enjoyable years. When once we said, "I can't," after gaining fitness and well-being through dedicated exercise, we say, "Don't just sit there, let's get moving."

A strong back and strong heart match one's courage and confidence, four natural byproducts of working out and regular lifting. And, though personally pleased, true ironheads don't brag about their accomplishments—one more modest attribute gained from solid cast-iron training.

Wait. I said I was gonna be brief.

Not all the fun was captured on the beaches of sunny California. There were the eight- and ten-story abandoned buildings in the old garment district of Manhattan. Somehow, we gained admittance to these deteriorating fire hazards and were dragged by chattering and screeching cables of old industrial lifts to forsaken levels high above alleys and dumpsters below.

After clearing a corner of over-turned benches, worktables and indeterminable debris, we settled in to serious photography. A white backdrop was hung in contrast to the dust and mold, and spider webs as thick as tapestries in a haunted house. The rats kept to themselves; I was more concerned with the warped floorboards that shook perceptibly as we traversed our surroundings, soldiers in a minefield.

The camera sat on its tripod, the lights and reflectors and umbrellas were in place and the champion stood on his mark, all objects precisely determined by strings with signifying knots in measured placements. The oil is smoothly applied after a hint of a pump is gained by flexing in place. Swell! Move from your mark, you get smudged and grimy, splintered and wounded, infected and quarantined. The trouble starts when a thirsty star asks for a slug of water. It's hot and stuffy in New York City in August. No water. It worsens when he has to go to the men's room. No plumbing.

No problem is too big or too small for a band of smiling bodybuilders.

"One, two, three and flex. Again, and this time, Dave, twist harder and don't forget to flex your legs. Jimmy, is he standing in the right spot? One, two, three and flex. That was good, Bomber. Once more, this is for a cover. Twist, bring your arms higher; flex your legs. NO, no, no! Caruso, you tell him! Twist, flex, arms higher, higher. Smile!"

I'll tell you this: No one got the poses and photographs like Joe Weider.

Once I stood in the center of Century Plaza, on the granite edge of a stunning water fountain. The size of a tennis court, the fountain adorned the center-divide of Century Boulevard and was framed by towering thirty-story glass-fronted office buildings to the east and west. Water gushed brilliantly toward the sky, and I nonchalantly busied myself while glowing with oil in my teal posing trunks waiting for Russ Warner to prepare his camera, position himself and position me. It was high noon — lunchtime, in the bustling, sophisticated business district of Beverly Hills, home of world finance and filmmaking. Traffic was heavy and animated. No problem, I'm cool. I've been stared at before.

"Yeah, you too, wise guy!!"

Oh, look. Russ is talking to some policemen who are pointing at me. Old friends, no doubt, but I refrain from waving. Rather than pump up, I try to look very small as I stroll through the slightly slimy shallow pool to the other side. Chilly. Halfway there I hear the whoop-whoop sound emergency vehicles make when they approach an intersection and want it cleared immediately. I return to my original post — dripping wet — and, as if responding to their signal, hit an overhead, double-arm biceps shot, a side back shot and a kneeling side chest. I'm Mr. America, after all. I bow and wait for the traffic to subside before I jaywalk and join them at their bleeping patrol car.

"Hi, guys. My name is Dave Draper."

I forget how it went after that. The human being has a weird way of going numb and blocking things out — playing dead — when under siege.

Crazy, man. Why did we do the stuff we did? Don Howorth, Larry Scott, Zane, Yorton, Labra, McArdle, Zabo, Eifferman, Sipes. The money?

No. Not the money. Sure, a few bucks would have paid some bills and broadened the smile, but no, not the dough.

The fame and glory? Such rewards circulated close to home and no one was profoundly impressed, least of all the champs. The brotherhood of recognition was quiet, almost silent. Fame and glory were as rewarding as the kiss of congratulations from the pretty girl in the miniskirt onstage.

I'll never forget the authentic thunder of applause and cheering in New York, but the fans in those days were there for the same reasons we were.

It was the doing it that was good.

And it's the doing it that continues to be good. None of us would change much if we were to do it all again. The smiles came when they weren't expected and they've lasted a long, long time.

Lift weights for fame, glory and money and you miss the point entirely.

If you don't understand what I'm saying, I can't explain it.

Dave Draper

AFTERWORD

by Dick Tyler

For some reason, I decided to go to a movie, a Saturday matinee. The theater was packed with screaming kids, there to see the first *Superman* film starring Christopher Reeve. The first part of the film was pure fun, with everyone laughing and enjoying the man of steel's legendary feats of strength. Then he takes the lovely Lois Lane for a flying trip around the New York skyline. The kids in the theater were jumping up and down, some pretending they were flying.

At last, Superman brings Lois back to her apartment. Dazzled by her flying experience, Lois asks just what he stands for. His answer: "Truth, justice and the American way."

"Oh, come on," says Lois sarcastically. This mirrored the great laughing reaction of the audience.

Now the camera came to a close shot of Superman's face. His eyes narrowed and he replied very simply, "Lois, I never lie."

The theater suddenly went silent. I could almost hear a pin drop.

At that point, a completely different perception took place. With the simplicity and sincerity of the statement—Lois, I never lie—the movie was transformed from a large production of a cartoon character into an epic journey in the battle of good against evil. It was the turning point of the film.

Another such example was the second *Rocky* film. Poor Rocky was out of shape for his upcoming championship fight, and his wife, who was always after him to quit fighting, was in a coma. To the great frustration of the audience, Rocky sits by her hospital bed, mumbling how much he loves her, when her eyes flutter open.

"Rocky," she whispers.

"Oh, honey, you're awake!" he says excitedly.

She motions for him to come closer and whispers one simple word, "Win."

With that, the famous Rocky theme thundered through the theater, and the audience was electrified. With a single word, what was a corny fight film became a classic. It was that film's turning point.

I have often felt that most successful endeavors revolve around a turning point that makes the common become uncommon and even great. This happened in bodybuilding with the advent of the first Mr. Olympia contest in New York.

It was not, however, the contest itself, but what led up to it. For years, bodybuilding contests were treated as little more than a freak show tacked to the end of a weightlifting meet, which might not end until the early morning hours.

When Steve Reeves starred in a film about Hercules in the late '50s, the public perception of bodybuilders began to change. While more and more gyms began to open, the world of bodybuilding was still a world unto itself. The public might look in wonder at the massive muscles of those who wore them, but they essentially had no concept of what they took to build.

They knew nothing of the hours and years of the smell of sweat, the clanging of heavy plates, the yells of training partners or the grunts of agony and pain to squeeze out one more rep. They knew nothing of sacrifices in a bodybuilder's personal life or the hours of sleep required or the diet and nutritional supplementation needed to get the most out of training. Only a true bodybuilder knew that.

The money has not been minted that would be sufficient to equal the value of the sacrifices needed to become a bodybuilding champion.

It wasn't until the early '60s when Joe Weider came up with the idea of having a competition to pit only the winners of major contests against each other that the bodybuilders themselves began to realize the importance and financial value of their enterprise. This was the birth of the first Mr. Olympia.

Little did anyone realize at the time, however, the real beginning of bodybuilding's turning point would be not in the Olympia contest itself, but in the Mr. America competition that was to precede it earlier that night.

For over a year, Weider had been extolling the wonders of a young bodybuilder named Dave Draper. He was a big kid with big muscles and had just won the Mr. New Jersey title. The problem was, he was just that, a kid with big muscles. All the photos we had of his training gave the perception of a muscular Pillsbury Doughboy. There was only a small amount of muscular separation and little definition, if any. To make things even more difficult, he had no tan. He made a white sheet look gray.

This is who Joe sent from New Jersey to California. One of my jobs at the time was to chronicle the bodybuilding scene in Southern California, and it was virtually dumped on me to build up this Blond Bomber to hero status as part of the job.

Fortunately, Dave turned out to be a nice guy and easy to talk with. Unfortunately, he never wanted to talk about himself. Since my job was to write about and build up the image of the Bomber, I was in trouble, as I was able to learn little about his training, and worse, just what on earth he looked like.

He always wore a baggy shirt with the sleeves turned to just above the wrists. From that, I was at least sure he had the most muscular wrists I'd ever seen. He trained at the then-Muscle Beach Gym, known to everyone as the Dungeon, always away from others, at times when few others were there...and always in heavy sweats. In other words, he was the best known unknown in bodybuilding—and wasn't about to be any help in changing that image.

For a while he hosted a local television station's show that played a bunch of the gladiator-type movies of the time. While we could see he was big, he never flexed or posed in any way, so it was no help to me at all.

I was beginning to panic. How could I write anything that was more myth that substance? However, my job was not so much to think as to do. So, I expanded on the things I knew: He was a great person to be around, and he was very strong.

In the meantime, Weider came up with the idea of the Mr. Olympia contest to determine the champion of champions. It was to be held at the Brooklyn Academy of Music, along with the Mr. America, Mr. Universe and Miss Americana competitions. And guess what? Dave Draper was to be an entrant in the Mr. America, his first competition since winning the Mr. New Jersey two years before.

To me and to everyone else, for Dave to enter the Mr. America competition was something of a joke. This was to be the greatest bodybuilding extravaganza ever presented. To take a virtually untested bodybuilder, build him into almost mythical proportions, and then offer him as some kind of freakish sacrifice was the height of cruelty. I felt sorry for Dave and the anxiety he was feeling.

Finally, it was the day of the contest. In New York, with Weider driving, we picked up Rick Wayne and Earl Maynard from their hotel. They had just arrived from England and were quite excited about competing that night. Soon the conversation turned to the contestants and, of course, to Dave Draper.

Rick, with his biting wit, began to ridicule Dave in not a very gentle way. "Oh, yes," he said, "The great Dave Draper, otherwise known in England as the great white whale."

I started to laugh.

Joe glanced over at me, "Wait till they see him, eh, Dick?"

I gulped. "Yeah, right," I replied weakly. "Just you wait."

That didn't slow Rick or Earl down a bit; they were on that proverbial roll. I only wish I'd had a tape recorder—this was funny stuff.

Joe was not amused.

The Brooklyn Academy is an enormous opera house. Just off the main stage was a dressing room that had been turned into a warm-up area, and in it, preparing for the prejudging, were just about all the great bodybuilders of that time. They were all either pumping like mad or practicing their posing in front of the mirrors. It was a writhing pit of muscles in the truest sense.

But where was the vaunted Blond Bomber? He was in a corner, warming up in a robe. Still no one knew what he looked like, but the moment of truth was fast approaching.

A few minutes before Dave was to go before the judges, Wayne approached him. "Look, Dave," he said, taunting. "I do believe you plan to pose with your robe on. Is that right?"

Dave didn't answer as others began to gather around. I watched and could tell the pain he was feeling. The others started kidding and telling him to take off the robe.

What happened next is hard to describe. It's one of those rare times when words fail to carry the message of what the eyes see.

Dave dropped his robe and for the first time we could see what he had been so carefully hiding. There was an audible gasp from those who gathered around.

Rick Wayne took a step backward and his jaw dropped.

I have personally never seen such a combination of raw power sculptured on such bronzed, separated and defined muscles.

Dave Draper went on to win the Mr. America, which began the turning point that culminated with Larry Scott winning the evening's Mr. Olympia contest. That night set the benchmark for all that would follow in the pages you just read, and the health and fitness advancements that came after.

Almost like Rocky, the audience leaned forward as Joe Weider whispered "Dave Draper," and the people were electrified. And, dear reader, as in *Superman*, what I've just told you is true because...I never lie.

Dick Tyler
Author, West Coast Bodybuilding Scene

www.ingramcontent.com/pod-product-compliance
Lightning Source LLC
Chambersburg PA
CBHW060043100426
42742CB00014B/2682

* 9 7 8 1 9 3 1 0 4 6 2 7 5 *